As I prepared to leave the Parc des Princes at the end of England's triumphant match over France, I looked out across the vast, empty, silent arena and realized then that my England days were finally over. It was a poignant moment as I gazed at all the debris scattered round the giant concrete stadium. After eight years of international rugby in all the great stadiums of the world, it was all over. But at least I had enjoyed a decent run and could console myself with the thought that I had come a long way from those far-off days when I began my senior career as the sixth team fullback at Fylde.

Thanks to Rugby

BILL BEAUMONT

ARROW BOOKS

Arrow Books Limited
17–21 Conway Street, London W1P 6JD

An imprint of the Hutchinson Publishing Group

London Melbourne Sydney Auckland
Johannesburg and agencies throughout
the world

First published by Stanley Paul 1982

Arrow edition 1983

© Bill Beaumont 1982

Made and printed in Great Britain
by The Anchor Press Ltd
Tiptree, Essex

ISBN 0 09 932300 1

To Hilary
Thank you for all the help
and support you have given to me,
and for the days and weekends you have been prepared
to spend on your own

Contents

Acknowledgements

This story is in my own words. It is, however, entirely due to Ian Robertson, rugby correspondent of the *Sunday Times*, that the 300,000 words originally spoken into endless hours of tape recordings have been structured, cut back to book length, and so carefully edited. Ian has devoted almost the whole summer to this work and I am particularly grateful to him for managing to produce a final script which keeps so exactly to my own thoughts and feelings.

I should also like to thank Jackie Valleday for proving herself the fastest typist in the west.

PHOTOGRAPHIC ACKNOWLEDGEMENTS

For permission to reproduce copyright photographs, the publishers would like to thank Mike Brett, Colorsport, *Daily Express*, *Daily Mirror*, E. D. Lacey, *Otago Daily Times*, the Press Association and the *Scotsman*.

1

Beginning at the End

Nine days after I left the pitch at Moseley with impaired vision following a bang on the head during the County Championship final in January 1982, I sat in the office of Dr Ray Lascelles, Consultant Neurologist at Manchester Royal Infirmary. It was the third similar injury I had received in the space of twelve months, but it was no worse than the previous two, and I regarded the neurological examination as a purely precautionary measure. Already I had had to drop out of the international against Ireland and I was now itching to play again.

Dr Lascelles's office was about half the size of the changing room at Twickenham with a few pictures sprinkled round the clinical white walls. I had just undergone five hours of extensive and exhaustive tests on my eyes, brain, head and reflexes, and I was completely confident I would be given the all-clear to resume my rugby career. Driving to the hospital that morning, I listened to the radio and heard I had been recalled to the England team and restored to the captaincy for the match against France. I was eagerly looking forward to training that evening and proving my fitness and general wellbeing that Saturday by playing for my club, Fylde, in a local derby against Orrell.

All day the nurses had been really kind and encouraging, assuring me at the end of each set of tests that I had done well and there was nothing to worry about. I had some preliminary tests on my eyesight to check my vision, my visual field and my pupil reflexes. Then I was

wired up with a series of electronic gadgets with electrodes all over my head to examine my brain, and I
underwent another series of tests to check that my eyes
and brain were working in harmony. Professor Isher-
wood gave me a brain scan, some x-rays of my head
from every conceivable angle, and underwent further
tests from a sophisticated machine which took serial
pictures of my brain at varying depths. A dye was in-
jected into a blood vessel in my arm and by following
the progress of the dye round my head, the specialist
could chart the contours of my brain.

At the end of it all, I was engulfed in a sea of buoyant
optimism. I could not possibly have been less prepared
for the eventual verdict when it was delivered in the
middle of the afternoon.

Dr Lascelles told me that I had come through all the
tests satisfactorily and he could see no long-term problems, but after detailed discussions with Dr Sarosh
Vakil, the neurologist who had examined me in Preston
the previous week, they had concluded I would be very
foolish to play rugby again. Another bang on the head
or the neck might well trigger off a similar reaction,
causing internal bleeding, which could lead to a stroke,
permanent loss of vision or brain damage. However
small such risks were, they did exist, and the full weight
of medical opinion confirmed that I should give up playing rugby.

I was completely taken aback, utterly dumbfounded.
I just sat there staring at the doctor, trying to collect my
thoughts. At no stage during the previous week had I
entertained even the remotest possibility that I might
have to retire on medical grounds. I found it desperately
difficult to comprehend the news.

My stomach started revolving at somewhere near the
speed of light and I felt physically sick. My whole way
of life for the previous ten years had suddenly disinte-
grated; my own little world had seemingly come to an
end. Training for rugby, playing rugby, travelling to
rugby matches and various squad sessions, spending

almost every summer abroad on a rugby tour – the game had dominated my entire existence. Since I first played for Fylde in 1971, everything I did revolved round rugby – my family life, my work and my social life. In fact, I used to reckon each year stretched, not from January to December, but from the start of the new rugby season in September through to April.

I remember saying, 'That's it, then, it's all over.' Dr Lascelles nodded. Like the proverbial drowning man clutching at straws, I summoned up the strength to ask just one question. 'If I was a young lad who had just been picked to play for England for the very first time, would you give exactly the same advice, or are you taking into account the fact that I have enjoyed a long run in the England team?' Without any hesitation, he repeated that the advice would be the same no matter the background. I would be risking serious permanent damage; to take such risks would be extremely unwise.

Visibly shaken, I shuffled out of the hospital and made for my car. Three months previously I had given up smoking, but as I passed a cigarette machine en route to the car park, I rammed in two fifty-pence pieces and instantly lit up. I smoked the whole packet of twenty, one after another, for the next couple of hours while I struggled to sort out the immediate future.

I stopped at a motorway service station to phone my wife, Hilary, to share the news. Hilary was shocked and deeply disappointed but it was not something we could discuss properly over the phone. She told me to hurry home so that we could try to sort everything out after dinner.

The next call I had to make was to the Lancashire rugby team secretary, Eddie Deasey. The Lancashire team were principal guests of honour at the Anglo-American Sporting Club in Manchester, and I was meant to be making the main speech. I explained to Eddie that a few very pressing problems had cropped up and I would not be able to attend the dinner. I asked him to apologize profusely for letting everyone down, promising to explain everything to him later. I think he guessed what the problem was, but he maintained a discreet silence, telling me not to worry and to look after myself.

Later that evening I phoned the chairman of the England selectors, Budge Rogers, to tell him the news and to withdraw from the team to play France. He was very sympathetic but said I had made the only sensible decision and he wished me well for the future.

I also managed to contact my parents in Barbados where they were on holiday. I knew my mother would panic if she heard what had happened first on the radio or television out there, or read about it in the local papers.

Finally, I contacted the current England coach who had guided the team to all its recent triumphs – Mike Davis. We had become very good friends over the years and more or less shared the same attitudes to life and to rugby. We talked for over an hour and he provided a welcome crutch to my crippled hopes. Understandably, we accepted the specialist's verdict and became quite emotional as we took a brief stroll down memory lane, recapturing some of the happier moments of my career. We talked about the great Lancashire teams, my first cap for England, the lean years at Twickenham, the unforgettable Grand Slam and two memorable tours with the British Lions. Such reminiscing did not necessarily make retirement any more palatable, but it provided a useful cushion against it, bringing home forcibly how fortunate I had been to taste the fruits of success. I would be able to savour those memories for ever. The feeling of numbness had gradually worn off and I managed to get a decent night's sleep.

If the visit that day signalled the end of my career, the beginning of the end came at Moseley in the final of the 1982 County Championship. Many of my greatest moments had come with Lancashire and as the county were celebrating their centenary year, I was desperately keen to beat the North Midlands. The first quarter of the match had been pretty scrappy, and although Lancashire were not playing at all well, we were gradually getting on top. Not for the first time in my life, I found myself trapped at the bottom of a ruck. In the hurly-burly of bodies, arms and legs flying in every direction, I was accidentally rewarded for my efforts with a stray knee landing a blow on the back of my head.

It was not a particularly severe clout and I played on blissfully unaware of any damage or side effects for a few minutes. But then, as I stood at a line-out, I could sense my vision faltering. I summoned onto the pitch our physiotherapist, Kevin Murphy, to examine me. I was having great difficulty in focusing on the player throwing the ball in at the line-out as the player and the ball just melted into the crowd in the background. I had a blind spot on the right-hand side of my peripheral vision where I was completely unable to distinguish the distance between myself and any given object.

This inability to discriminate exact distances and shapes in one particular area, in this case the general field of vision on my right-hand side, had happened before. If it did not clear up in the next few minutes I knew I would have to leave the pitch. The impaired vision persisted and ten minutes before half time I left the field of play, unwittingly for the very last time.

With the England–Ireland match only seven days away, I did not want to appear too badly hurt, but I had had similar problems several times during the previous decade. My local doctor, Dr Billy Wood, who came straight to the dressing room, knew my history inside out. During my early years at Fylde, he reckoned I had been too brave for my own good; I had visited him suffering from concussion over twenty times between 1971 and 1976. Broken down into simple statistics, I had been concussed three or four times every year for a period of six seasons. I would wake up the next morning with a splitting headache, as if I had a wicked hangover, except that the previous night I had not drunk any alcohol. Billy Wood knew I could not go on absorbing these blows for ever, and insisted that I undergo a full neurological examination.

The Lancashire team doctor, Noel Atkinson, was equally cheerful and encouraging as I lay groggily in the changing room. 'I'll tell you something for nothing – you certainly won't play against Ireland next week, that's for sure.'

I summoned up enough energy to blurt out a brief reply. 'That's what you think, but I don't know what the hell you're worried about. I'm feeling fine now and I'll be perfectly okay tomorrow and a hundred per cent fit to face Ireland.'

Hilary came in to see how I was. She gave my confidence another boost by telling me that I looked absolutely ghastly, she had never seen me look so pale and haggard. A specialist from Preston, Dr Chris Foulkes, came in to check my condition, and it was he who diagnosed the trouble as lack of visual discrimination rather than double or blurred vision or concussion.

I was aware that I was rather befuddled because of what happened when I went for a bath. The large communal bath in the changing room was half-filled with piping hot water which would have reached a suitable temperature an hour later when the match was over. But I had first use and I remember nearly burning to death as I turned a delightful shade of salmon pink. Relying heavily on instinct, I knew that if I added cold water to regulate the temperature, the bath would be lukewarm for the rest of the lads at the end of the match, so, a rather pathetic figure, I washed with great haste in this bubbling inferno, in order that the team could enjoy a hot bath later on. Feeling reasonably refreshed, I then returned to the tunnel to watch Lancashire win.

I was in no state to join the celebrations that night. Hilary drove me home soon after the final whistle. That evening I suffered from tingling sensations in my tongue, pins and needles down my left-hand side and some difficulty stringing words together. This was the third time in a year I had experienced such sensations, and I agreed with Billy Wood that I should have a check-up.

Curiously enough, although I felt pretty rough the next morning, I went off to Manchester to record the BBC quiz programme, 'A Question of Sport'. I may have lost a few neurons at Moseley, but it didn't seem to matter, as partnered by Lucinda Prior-Palmer and Frank Stapleton we recorded a handsome victory. I returned home in good heart and, full of hope, ready to square up to Dr Sarosh Vakil the next day.

I must confess I was a bit shaken on the Monday morning when I turned up for work to find two full television camera crews, one from the BBC and one from ITV, waiting to interview me about my impending retirement. I gave them each a few quotes, saying I was feeling fine and was off to hospital to get the all-clear for the Irish international. When I arrived at Preston Royal Infirmary, the hospital was crawling with a dozen photographers and journalists from every national paper. I did not relish a confrontation at that particular moment so I slipped in through a side door unnoticed.

Dr Vakil is a portly, friendly, entertaining neurologist at Preston Royal Infirmary. He is also a very sharp, quick-witted person who easily saw through my smoke screen. I desperately wanted to play against Ireland and I did everything in my power to persuade Dr Vakil to give me a clean bill of health. I did not actually lie to him, but I suppose I did withhold a wide range of facts which he would have found interesting and illuminating.

I admitted under crossfire that I had been concussed a couple of times in the early seventies, but stressed these were not serious incidents – I had not actually had to miss any matches because of them. So far, so good. Unfortunately, the two recent and more serious injuries raised grave doubts about my immediate future.

In January 1981 at Twickenham, about twenty minutes from the end of the Calcutta Cup match, I received a crack on the back of my head after catching the ball from a kick-off. Everything was fine for about four or five minutes, but then my vision went to pieces. Although I felt ghastly and was in a desperate way, I decided to stay on because we had already used our second row forward replacement when Bob Hesford took over from Nick Jeavons early in the match. After the game I lay down for an hour in the changing room, recovering sufficiently to attend the dinner in the evening. I had an attack of pins and needles down the left-hand side affecting my arm, hand and leg, and I also found my tongue suffered from intermittent tingling sensations. I stayed clear of alcohol but surfaced the next morning with a horrific headache.

I did not tell Dr Vakil about all these symptoms, although they were relevant, but I was more forthcoming when we dealt with my next knock as I knew he had detailed notes about my trip to Beziers. In August 1981, I accompanied Lancashire on a pre-season tour to France and although I had to return home on business after the first match in Agen, I flew back for the game in Beziers against a French Select XV. The match began at nine o'clock in the evening and with a couple of minutes of the game remaining I jumped up to catch a kick ahead. As I came down with the ball, I received an almighty crack on the back of my head which knocked me senseless. One of the French players must have accidentally mistaken my head for the ball, and tried to kick it about two miles down the road.

After the match I was in a dreadful state with all the symptoms that had recently plagued me – impaired vision, tingling tongue, pins and needles and speech difficulties. I knew what I wanted to say but I was slurring my speech and just could not manage to force out the right words.

About one o'clock in the morning I was taken to the local hospital where I was examined by a specialist who had been dragged out of bed specially for the occasion. Through John Benn-Lewis, our interpreter, I was informed that I had the neck of a forty-year-old and should give up rugby at once. Well, I reckoned that the world was full of forty-year-old people managing perfectly well with forty-year-old necks; it did not seem to do them any harm. So, after a couple of weeks' break, I decided to seek a second opinion in England. In early September I visited a top neck specialist in Liverpool and after a series of x-rays he pronounced me fit enough to continue playing.

With all this background information, Dr Vakil was less easy to convince. He informed me that I must not play against Ireland that Saturday and I must return for further tests the following Monday. He pointed out a dark patch on my brain scan which, though consistent with the knock I had incurred at Moseley, could be the result of an old knock; if it did not go in the ensuing few days, its effects would be more serious. I left the hospital optimistic that I would be back playing for Fylde against Orrell in a fortnight.

Dr Vakil, on the other hand, was more pessimistic. He spent the next few days researching my past. Inevitably, he came up with a fairly accurate total of the number of concussions I had sustained throughout my career, and he also turned up a couple of incidents I had neglected to mention.

Following two cases of severe concussion in 1975 and 1977, I had visited another neurologist, Dr Ken Tutton, in Preston. I was suffering from all the problems which were to become my trade marks – impaired vision, tingling tongue, pins and needles and slurred speech. When Dr Vakil unearthed this information and Dr Lascelles confirmed that the dark patch on the brain scan was still there, my playing days were numbered. In retrospect, I appreciate that the doctors arrived at the only possible decision. The facts were displayed to me so forcibly that I accepted their findings without any hesitation, though with a great deal of sadness.

The risk of paralysis, minor or major brain damage, or permanent loss of vision was obviously unacceptable, so I was incensed by what I thought was a wild and irresponsible article which appeared in the *Sunday Tele-*

19

graph suggesting that I had made the wrong decision, and should continue playing. The RFU were equally infuriated by what they also considered to be an ill-informed, potentially dangerous article and their strong condemnation of it was published in the *Sunday Telegraph* the following week.

The announcement that my career was over was given to the press by the RFU first thing on Tuesday morning (9 February) and I waited in anticipation for the inevitable avalanche of journalists and photographers to disturb the normal peace and calm of Chorley. I was not disappointed.

The television and camera crews duly arrived from the BBC and ITV. There were also representatives of local and national radio, both BBC and commercial, clutching their tape recorders, and about twenty journalists from the national papers, plus a dozen photographers. I had already told my colleagues at work what had happened and warned them that I would have to sacrifice most of the day to giving interviews to the media. None the less, I was staggered at the interest shown – a steady convoy of cars came and went all day. I still find it hard to understand the extent of the coverage devoted to my story.

However, I was pleased to talk to every reporter, believing that once I had set the record straight that would, in every sense, be the end of it. By late Tuesday evening I was emotionally and physically drained and was understandably a trifle annoyed when a couple of journalists phoned to ask if they could arrange to photograph me watching Fylde play Orrell on the Saturday. I reckoned they had all had their pound of flesh by then and I rejected the request for two reasons: I thought such coverage would take the limelight away from the two clubs and, anyway, it was all a bit macabre. To their credit, they readily accepted the situation, as did the BBC, which made a similar bizarre request to film me watching an ordinary club match at Fylde.

In the event, I was able to enjoy a smashing game of

rugby in peace and quiet. Fylde had not been having a very good season and I was desperate for the lads to do well. Before the game I wished them luck and to my sheer delight they played their best match all season to record a dramatic and rather unexpected win. I went into the changing room afterwards feeling very emotional and thanked them all for their magnificent effort. I told them it meant a lot to me and the captain, Mick Weir, said that the team had done it for me as their way of saying 'Thanks for the memory'. I was deeply moved and terribly proud and we adjourned to the bar to wallow in a little nostalgia.

Later that evening, I was overwhelmed by a marvellous gesture from the Orrell Club, traditionally fierce local rivals. They presented me with a magnificent cutglass whisky decanter and made me an honorary member of their club in recognition, I suppose, of all the memorable battles we had fought during the previous twelve years. It was certainly a great way to end the most traumatic week of my life.

The next Saturday I was delighted to accept an invitation to join the BBC Television commentary team in Paris for the France–England match and thoroughly enjoyed myself. The previous match against Ireland at Twickenham had been a strange affair. I had been invited down to London by the Rugby Football Union to join the team as a guest, but because I was not playing I felt quite lost. Before the match I hung around inside the dressing room like a little boy with his nose pressed against the window of a sweet shop, looking at all the enticing goodies but knowing they were not for him. I realized then that one was either a player or not a player; if I was not actually playing I would much rather not be there.

I wished Steve Smith, the new captain, luck, and left. Smithy is one of the great characters of the game. He is an outstanding player with a fantastic sense of humour and we had become good friends during our years together with Lancashire and England. When I phoned to tell him my bad news about retiring, he was typically sympathetic in his own amusing way. 'Christ, Bill, you shouldn't complain. After five hours of tests, the doctors actually have proof that you do have a tiny brain hiding away inside that big, dull head. Who would have believed it? Mind you, it's a great shame that having found a brain, you've now destroyed it.'

However, he went on to point out that I might have had to retire ten years earlier with nothing to look back on but a couple of games for Lancashire and the thrill of a decade on the Fylde selection committee. Put that way, I certainly had to count my blessings.

The Irish match was a disaster. England lacked control even though the enthusiasm and energy were there. Smithy summed it up best at the post-match press conference. 'We spent eighty minutes running round like headless chickens.' When I went back to the dressing room, the lads turned to me and said, 'Here's the first rat off the sinking ship.'

Despite this setback, a win over France was not considered an impossibility and I was looking forward to making my debut as a summarizer on television with an England success. Before the match I was doing an interview on the pitch with David Coleman for 'Grandstand' when the England team arrived. They were joking and waving on the pitch and they invited me into the dressing room afterwards, but I gracefully declined, remembering the feeling of anticlimax I had experienced hanging around in the dressing room before the Irish match.

The French had not picked a very well-balanced side and England produced their best performance of the season to win fairly comfortably. I thoroughly enjoyed my little contributions on television and with the news of the Scottish defeat in Dublin, felt pleased for Ireland that they had captured the Triple Crown.

I finished all my television commitments about an hour after the final whistle. As I prepared to leave, I looked out across the vast, empty, silent arena at Parc des Princes and realized then that my England days were finally over. It was a poignant moment as I gazed at all the debris scattered round the giant concrete stadium. After eight years of international rugby in all the great stadiums of the world, it was all over. But at least I had enjoyed a decent run and could console myself with the thought that I had come a long way from those far-off days when I began my senior career as the sixth team fullback at Fylde.

2

The Early Days

One is not just born to be the sixth team fullback at Fylde. One has to train, practise and play for nine years at school before managing to achieve that rare accolade. My story began in Preston on 9 March 1952, when Ron and Joyce Beaumont became the proud parents of a 9-lb baby boy. For a baby born one month premature by caesarean section, that was a very healthy weight. The story nearly ended shortly afterwards as I was not given all that good a chance of surviving until the end of the month. After a few days I contracted pneumonia and my parents had me baptized in hospital because they were not at all confident of my pulling through.

The paediatrician, Dr Gordon Hesling, informed my parents that he had seen lots of other seven-day-old babies with pneumonia in a worse state than me survive, but he had also seen plenty of tiny tots a lot better off die. He said there was a new, dangerous and expensive drug on the market called Chloromycetin and he would seek permission from the Ministry of Health to prescribe this for me. Within a fortnight I recovered but I remained a sickly child.

I spent the first three weeks of my sojourn on earth in hospital and just when I seemed to have shaken off pneumonia and was ready to go home, my mother noticed an alarming sequence of events on my daily medical chart. Fed – vomited. Fed – vomited. Fed – vomited. Fed – vomited. Mother knew at once what the problem was. Our family had had a chequered history of people

suffering from a horrible condition called pyloric stenosis. In simple, layman's terms, a victim of this illness
suffers from a narrowing of the exit to the stomach.
Anything swallowed reaches the stomach, but goes no
farther. Instead, it is all vomited back up. Obviously,
with nothing being digested, if this condition had been
allowed to continue I would have surely died. In only
three weeks my weight had dropped from 9 lb to under
6 lb – a loss of over a third of my original body weight.

My uncle had been one of the first babies with this
condition to survive when he was born with pyloric
stenosis in India shortly after the First World War. My
grandmother fed him for twelve months with a tiny salt
spoon, about a quarter of the size of a teaspoon, and he
managed to digest tiny quantities of sustenance in small
doses given at regular intervals.

By 1952, the doctors were able to perform an operation
to sort out the trouble although a general anaesthetic on
a three-week-old mite poses problems of its own, apart
from the surgical complications. Happily the operation
was a complete success and I had negotiated my second
crisis.

The trouble did not end there though. A few days
later my stitches turned septic and I was back popping
a few more pills before the paediatrician wisely suggested
that my parents take me home before anything else went
wrong. It would be nice to report that all was sweetness
and light after that, but I had two other little setbacks
to face.

I had developed, if that is the right word, a pigeon
chest and I was also asthmatic. My father sorted out the
pigeon chest by performing recommended exercises and
home physiotherapy on me every day for the first two
years of my life. The idea was to move my arms about
and generally exercise my chest to build it up and this
treatment and kind parental doting paid rich dividends.
The doctor was astounded how I had improved so dramatically in two years. The asthma cleared up when I
went to boarding school at the age of eight and since

then I have quite closely resembled a normal human being.

Nevertheless, I owe a huge debt of gratitude to Dr Hesling. Although we had no contact with him between 1954 and 1975, my mother wrote to him when I won my first cap for England. She reminded him of the puny little baby who caused him such anxiety in 1952 and wondered what the odds would have been then of that wretched little creature going on to play lock forward for England.

My family lived in a small mill town called Adlington near Chorley in Lancashire and I was the middle child of three. My sister, Alison, is eighteen months older than I am and my brother Joe is four years younger; I spent most of my early days playing with Alison. We have always been a close-knit family and still all live and work in and around Chorley, meeting regularly as a family unit.

My father played college rugby at Cambridge and then played for Fylde, and he has always taken a keen interest in my career. Thankfully, he has never pushed himself into the limelight and I have been very grateful for the fact that he is perfectly content to sup his ale unnoticed in the corner of the bar and has never had any desire to share the spotlight. It has been reassuring to have had his loyal support during the past fifteen years.

My mother's main concern each Saturday was the universal maternal hope that I didn't get injured. I think she has tempered the disappointment that I have had to retire with a great deal of relief that she won't have to worry about me getting any more whacks on the rugby pitch every week.

Although the first two years of my life had been quite eventful, during the next two my mother reckons I only got into the same amount of trouble as any normal wild, mischievous, tearaway would. At the age of four I found that all good things come to an end – I started school. The first stage of my education took place at an establishment with the most unpretentious of names – it was simply called the Council School. Every child has his or her favourite time at school and I was no exception. I thoroughly enjoyed the breaks. When the bell sounded for a break, we would rush out into the playground and play soccer until the next bell tolled to summon us back to the grim realities of the classroom. From all the evidence I've been able to collect from parents, teachers, and the end-of-year reports, there seemed very little danger of my turning into a book worm or an academic recluse. My appetite for such exciting adventures as the alphabet and addition and subtraction was strictly limited and I was not particularly skilful at disguising my lack of interest in such pursuits.

In the hope that I might expand my educational horizons beyond a useful working knowledge of the game of soccer, my parents decided to send me when I was eight years old to a prep school – Cressbrook School in Kirkby Lonsdale.

My father took me along for my interview at Cressbrook and that was the first time I ever touched a rugby ball. I spotted a large wicker basket full of balls outside the headmaster's study and took this as a healthy sign of the shape of things to come. I picked one up and, as the headmaster, Mr David Donald, came out of his room, hastily threw it back into the basket. He took my interest in the rugby ball as an encouraging sign. By getting my name right, I sailed through the interview.

My abiding memory of the school was being forced to have a cold bath every morning throughout the winter and spring terms. In the summer term, glory be, we had the thrilling dilemma of choosing either a cold bath or swimming a length of the freezing outdoor swimming pool. As if that was not enough, the school also had the perverse fetish of embarking regularly on long cross-country walks. I arrived at the school on a Friday and on the Saturday, after, of course, my cold bath, I was dragged six miles across fields, over hills and down dales. I wondered what the blazes was going on.

Surprisingly, although my system never quite accepted the cruel shock of the cold bath every morning, I enjoyed my days at Cressbrook School enormously, with its strong emphasis on the outdoor life and sport. The head boy at the school when I arrived was a blond-haired boy called John Spencer. We all lived in his reflected glory during the next few years as he went on to play for Sedbergh, England Schoolboys, Cambridge University and, eventually, England.

Initially, we played soccer in the autumn and rugby in the spring term, but later on we concentrated on rugby right through the winter. The master in charge of the rugby side in my first season went on the shrewd principle that the eight biggest lads were made into forwards and the other seven became backs. Thus, I spent the term as a prop forward, although by the end of it I realized there must be a more glamorous position in which I could play. The next season, would you believe, the fly half of the Cressbrook School Juniors was W. B. Beaumont.

What is even more incredible is that no one tumbled to the fact that my style was not based exclusively along the lines of Cliff Morgan, Jackie Kyle and the other fly half heroes of the late fifties – I remained at fly half for the next three seasons. It will come as no surprise to those people horrified at the vision of Bill Beaumont bursting onto his scrum half's pass, then jinking through the opposing defence to score a spectacular try, that I was actually a much more promising cricketer than a rugby player. I dare say the idea of Phil Bennett and myself being the two British Lions fly halves in New Zealand in 1977 does seem a trifle far fetched.

In my final year at Cressbrook I was made captain of the rugby team, but I only played a couple of matches before breaking an ankle. This accident, it will be noted, did not occur in the school library by my falling off a ladder trying to reach a book on the top shelf in vigorous pursuit of my studies. I was no more enthusiastic to eat from the tree of knowledge than I had been hitherto, but none the less I was making satisfactory progress. My comeback to the games field was unfortunately delayed because I broke the plaster on my leg while playing yet another impromptu game of soccer on the tennis court. Nothing so trivial as a broken leg was allowed to curtail my sporting activities.

I spent my last two summers at Cressbrook in the first eleven disguised as an opening batsman and I met with a fair amount of success. Cricket, like pyloric stenosis, runs in the family. At that time my uncle, Joe Blackledge, was captain of Lancashire. As a special treat as a youngster I was occasionally taken along to watch Lancashire when they played county matches at Blackpool.

I also supported Blackburn Rovers soccer side and our next-door neighbour in Adlington, Sydney Croston, used to take me along to most of the home games. In those days Rovers had a few decent players – Bryan Douglas and Ronnie Clayton, who both played for England, and Derek Dougan, who went on to play for Northern Ireland. Blackburn was in the First Division then and I used to see some first-class matches. I always remember being heartbroken when Rovers lost to Wolverhampton Wanderers in the FA Cup Final in 1960.

The following year I went to Wembley to watch my first major sporting event – a soccer international in which England beat Scotland by a small matter of nine goals to three. My next big treat was in my last year at Cressbrook when our rugby side had an away match in Edinburgh on the Friday afternoon before the Calcutta Cup match. It was quite an occasion for a bunch of youngsters to set off for the first time in their lives to a real away match played in a foreign country, stay overnight in a hotel, and watch a live rugby international. We arrived at Murrayfield at midday on the Saturday and plonked ourselves down on our seats in the enclosure, soaking up the atmosphere for three hours until the kick-off.

I relished every moment and it made a deep impression

on me, although never for a second did I ever dream
that one day I would play an international on that pitch.
I did have the audacity to dream in my more romantic
moments that one day, perhaps, Boycott and Beaumont
would open for England at Old Trafford, but there was
precious little conviction behind the fantasy. The only
black spot on a wonderful day was the result at Murrayfield – Scotland won by 15 points to 6 – and that put
a mild damper on the return journey.

Looking back on my four years at Cressbrook, the
highlight of my rugby career came in a match against
Bow School from Durham. They were the crack prep
school in the north. Not only did they finish the season
undefeated, they only conceded 3 points all year. Those
3 points were scored by the Cressbrook School fly half,
W. B. Beaumont, with a drop goal in open play –
right-footed as it so happened!

In 1965, at the end of a lively and interesting period
of my life, the time had come to leave Cressbrook. The
headmaster told my parents that I would be remembered
as one of the roughest, toughest boys to have passed
through the school. He added, 'Roughest in the nicest
possible way, of course' – whatever that meant. He said
I was one of those unfortunate wretches that trouble
seemed to court. Through no fault of my own, trouble
tended to follow me around. I recall explaining to him
one day that it was just desperately bad luck that I
happened to be leaning against the huge plate-glass window of the local sweet shop when it splintered into a
thousand pieces and I plunged through the gap. It could
have happened to anyone.

Next stop was Ellesmere College in Shropshire where
the headmaster was the former England wing forward
Ian Beer. I arrived bright-eyed and bushy tailed, claiming to be a goal-kicking fly half. I survived in that dual
role for three years in the under-14, under-15 and
under-16 teams. We actually had a very good side. We
won far more games than we lost, and we were very well
coached by the school chaplain, a Scotsman called

Maurice Gray. He coached us right through the school and, as a prop forward himself, he realized after three seasons that I was not a natural fly half and he changed my position – to fullback!

I spent my last two seasons at school as the last line of defence, but we did not enjoy a very successful run. I don't think I was especially to blame for our sudden reversal of form, but my father kept assuring me that I would never be a back of any description and certainly not a fullback. Curiously enough, we did have one outstanding forward in that team – a flanker called Mark Keyworth. Ironically, six years later, in 1976, we were both in the full England side and, following on from our disastrous record at Ellesmere College, England lost all four internationals that year and Keyworth disappeared from the national squad. He returned as substitute for the Calcutta Cup game of 1980.

Although the happiest memories of my school days were the countless hours spent on the rugby field and the cricket pitch, I did manage to scrape together my fair share of O levels, much to everyone's surprise and delight. But as my end-of-term reports were always less than flattering and it was generally acknowledged I was bone idle, my father took me away before my A-level year and suggested I go to Salford College of Technology. It was the only college of further education he knew where the students were subjected to a minimum of academic pressure and where they were never set any homework. To me it sounded like paradise and I willingly agreed to study for a diploma in business studies and textile technology.

Sport still dominated my life during the two years I studied – I use that word in the loosest possible sense – at Salford. I played rugby for the college every Wednesday and I played for one of the lower teams at Fylde each Saturday. In the summer I played cricket for Chorley in the Northern League, and I became close friends with another player in the team – Paul Mariner. As the two youngest guys in the side, we used to knock around together quite a lot and had some good times. Since those distant days, I have closely followed Paul's soccer career with Ipswich and England. We have always kept in touch, although it is over a decade since we went our separate ways.

My cricket continued to flourish at Salford and I continued to enjoy it, but my rugby career was to take a dramatic change of direction.

3

Fylde

My senior rugby career began with Fylde, and the story of the first week was not one of unrestricted and unqualified triumph. Our family had enjoyed a strong link with the club stretching back to the early part of the century when my grandfather was a keen member. My father continued the tradition, playing occasionally in the first team but mostly in the seconds, and I had always hoped that one day I would be able to follow in their footsteps.

Right at the outset my father sent a letter to the secretary, Arthur Bell, asking if I could become a playing member and pointing out that I had been fullback in the 1st XV at Ellesmere College for two years. He admitted that I had grown alarmingly during the past two years and because of my size I was inevitably a shade slow. Although I could welly the ball a fair distance, it was his opinion that I might well eventually end up in the forwards.

I doubt that my father ever imagined how expeditiously Fylde would execute those sentiments. I turned up for my first training session at six o'clock in the evening as I had been informed that training was from six o'clock onwards. I did not appreciate that most of the other players had jobs, families and had to travel several miles to reach the ground. Bodies did not begin staggering into the club house till nearer seven o'clock. Not that I was bored in the intervening hour. I had borrowed my mother's car for the evening and, being rather shy and a little anxious about my first night with new faces at a new club, in my excitement and panic I had locked the car door with the keys still inside. For a quarter of an hour I had circumnavigated the car, desperately hoping for a miracle, but at the end of a whole lot of wishful thinking, the car doors remained firmly locked and the keys were still inside. I remember feeling very sheepish about the whole episode. My chances of creating a favourable impression on my first appearance were fast receding.

However, when some of the veteran campaigners pitched up, they quickly put me at my ease. People were nearly trampled to death in the rush to offer me their kit to train. The lucky person nearest to me in size could then slope off to the bar with a clear conscience and a warm glow from his beneficent Christian act of kindness in lending me his kit. As it transpired such generosity was not needed. Someone produced a piece of wire and my worldly knowledge increased as one of the guys managed to open the door and retrieve my keys and kit.

Life took a sharp turn for the better after that initial hiccup and I was selected on the Saturday at fullback for the 6th XV against a local side called Burnage. This was my opportunity to display all my skills and show everyone just what sort of a fullback I was. I did exactly that and, as a result, never played behind a scrum again in my entire career! One of the shrewd judges at Fylde, Alan Townsend, who used to spend a lot of time coaching the junior sides, took one look at me in that game and broke the news to me that he could see no future for me as a fullback – or indeed any sort of back. I was sentenced to be a 'donkey' for the rest of my playing days. We actually won that match, but ten years of training and practising fullback and fly-half skills were rendered obsolete and the following week I played for the 6th at flank forward.

I spent the next three months in the 6th as a flanker and thoroughly enjoyed it once I was acclimatized. However, I quickly twigged that most of my playing colleagues were not necessarily fired with the same burning ambition to advance to the 5th as I was. In general, the team comprised mostly the older members of the club who had seen better days and who were now content to see out what remained of their careers languishing in their own nostalgia in the 6th. They were in no danger of being dropped because there was no seventh team and they had no desire to win promotion. It was almost a club within a club and while it was a fascinating experience to watch these wily warriors every week, unlike them, I did not want to spend the rest of my life in the 6th.

Therein lay the crux of the problem. They liked having me in their side. In the intriguing world of coarse rugby it was a great bonus to have one young, fit, enthusiastic workaholic in the team. For the fading stars of the 6th, it was manna in the wilderness to have someone who could play flat out for eighty minutes without stopping for a cigarette, and who relished tackling, falling on the ball, rucking and mauling and all the other chores of a rugby forward. Now that they had one, they did not intend to lose him easily. I played my heart out every week only to be rewarded with reselection for the 6th the following week. I would have loved to have been a fly on the wall at the Monday evening selection meetings.

'Ah yes, Chairman, I'm glad you asked me about young Beaumont. He is doing adequately and he's very keen but, of course, he's very inexperienced and I think he's learning an enormous amount from playing every week with so many really experienced men. I should think about five years with us in the 6th and he could be ready for better things.'

I should imagine the report from the captain of the 6th went something along those lines. He was the sole selector for our team, but we used to travel to away matches with the 3rd and they had a real live selector all of their own called Roy Gartside. He would watch almost all of the 3rd's game but he would usually stroll across to take in ten or fifteen minutes of the 6th's match to check on the form of any of the players under pensionable age. •

Normally, I would spend the match being asked to jump at every line-out both on the opposition ball and on our own; I would be involved in every back-row move at the scrums and I would be given the ball to set up all the rucks and mauls. But, funnily enough, for a quarter of an hour every second week at our away matches, when Roy Gartside was on the touch line, I was totally ignored by my team mates. The ball was never thrown to me, there were no back-row moves and I was used exclusively as a decoy. I was virtually frozen out of the match by the machiavellian tactics of the 6th team junta. Doubtless, Roy Gartside had the impression that I was either useless, lazy or did not even exist.

I was beginning to believe that I might grow old in the nethermost regions of the club when my big break came. The 3rd XV were short of players prepared to travel to Newcastle for their annual safari and binge to play Percy Park 3rd and I was offered the chance to join this expedition. My mother asked me what time I would be home and I estimated around 11 p.m. or midnight at the latest. I met the team bus in Preston and off we set on the biggest rugby adventure of my career thus far.

In those dim and distant days I received £3 a week spending money and I decided to take a third of my entire week's revenue on the trip to Newcastle. Clutching my pound note in a sweaty paw, I boarded the bus and, not knowing any of the players, settled down at the front to avoid the card school and conserve my energy and my pound note for the day ahead. We duly arrived, played the game and won but, to my surprise, we did not all leap back on board the coach after a bite to eat to return post haste to Lancashire with the good news. The gang felt an obligation to try to celebrate our victory by drinking Newcastle dry or at worst be sick in the attempt. I soon discovered my pound was not going to last all that long. The seasoned travellers had a whip-round to ensure I could partake of some liquid refresh-

ment in the ensuing six hours, and I was able happily
to gargle my way through the evening. After undertaking
some serious drinking in the Percy Park club house, we
adjourned to a pub in the heart of seedy dockland called,
somewhat appropriately, The Jungle. There the local
lads regaled us with macabre tales of the gangland knif-
ings which were a daily occurrence in that area.

I was horrified by these stories but sought suitable
solace in the local beer. By closing time I had had a
right skinful. I crawled onto the bus and curled up on
the back seat where I thought I might be able to steal
forty winks. However, the regulars had other ideas and
a dreadful cacophony of noise, purporting to be singing,
accompanied us all the way to Scotch Corner where we
stopped for a meal. I looked at my watch and was just
about able to work out it was half past two in the
morning. At that moment, despite the enticing counter-
attractions of pie and chips on the motorway, I had a
splendid and noble brainwave. It seemed like the perfect
opportunity to phone home and explain that I had been
unavoidably detained and might well be back a trifle
late.

My mother answered the phone. I blurted out the
general message that we had reached Scotch Corner.
Although I might be home a little later than planned,
there was no need for her to worry as I would be safely
home in about three or four hours' time. She turned to
my father, dug him in the ribs to wake him up, and told
him that his son, without any doubt whatsoever, had
just played his very last game of rugby. With that she
defiantly rang off.

Fortunately she mellowed during the next few days
and I was given a stay of execution. I had played quite
well against Percy Park and had a memorable trip. That
journey has now passed into the club's folklore and we
still raise the topic from time to time even now, but the
greatest significance to me was the fact that I was able
to retain my place in the 3rd and soon win promotion
to the 2nd.

My attitude to rugby hardened at this time, too. The 3rd took the game much more seriously than the 6th. I embarked on a course of weight training and, determined to become much fitter, trained a lot harder.

A few weeks later, around Christmas 1969, I changed from flank to lock forward and found myself chosen for the 2nd. I stayed in the 2nd at lock until the end of the season, but at the beginning of the next winter I switched to prop in the belief that I was too short for the line-out. I was demoted to the 3rd for a month to learn the intricacies of the front row, before returning to the 2nd, en route to my first-team debut at prop against Waterloo in November 1970.

The Fylde hooker at that time was a pig farmer called Billy Baxter who never trained and turned up for matches about three minutes before kick-off stinking to high heaven and with a fair smattering of pig muck clinging to him. Although we had not had any time to practise before the match, we survived intact, winning our own ball and also the match 13–nil, but I was dropped for the next game because the prop I had replaced had recovered from injury.

I was injured myself shortly afterwards, tearing my ankle ligaments, and I did not play again that season, missing the next four months. I resumed in September 1971 at lock forward in the 3rd and by early November I had worked my way back to the 1st XV for the match against New Brighton. Within two years I had established myself in the Fylde side and the following year I won my first cap for Lancashire.

I was only dropped by Fylde once after that New Brighton game and that was on Boxing Day 1971 for the annual match against Preston Grasshoppers. Roger Uttley was home for Christmas from Newcastle, where he was a student and played for Gosforth. As Fylde was his original club, he was selected in my place. It was a real blow to me at the time but it encouraged me to redouble my efforts to become a fitter, stronger and better player, and I enjoyed my rugby a lot more as a result.

In the early seventies, Fylde had a useful back division with a tremendous scrum half, Brian Ashton, and a fast powerful wing in Tony Richards. Both were unlucky not to win caps for England and they were outstanding at club level. Brian went with England on the short tour to Australia in 1975 and he would certainly have been capped out there, but his wife had a miscarriage and he had to return home before the first Test.

Our pack lacked any such stars and it was hard work every week to win sufficient ball to give the backs a fair chance to run. I worked flat out all the time because this was the only way I knew, but I took an enormous number of knocks in those early days and suffered regularly from severe headaches. We did not have a big enough or experienced enough pack to protect individuals. As I grew older and began playing county and international rugby, I must confess I quite often found it frustrating playing at Fylde. I often wished some of the other players had been as committed and dedicated as I was and I occasionally found their lackadaisical approach very annoying. But, at the end of the day, it is an amateur sport and everyone is free to put as much or as little into the game as he chooses. I have never had any regrets that I spent my entire playing career with a so-called unfashionable club. There is a great deal more to rugby than simply playing the game and I have cherished the camaraderie and friendliness of the club throughout the past ten years.

The club is full of great people and two men typify the general attitude. Mel Whittle and Peter Makin are two of the hardest-working committee men imaginable. It is the unstinting efforts of people like them, in clubs all over the country, that allow the game not only to survive, but to flourish.

I had offers from other clubs in the area from time to time and briefly considered moving, but I would like to think that I am a fairly loyal, dependable person and I look back on my time at Fylde with great pleasure and satisfaction. We had as good a fixture list as any of the other clubs I might have been tempted to join and we won our fair share of games every year. Furthermore, the social side of our club would take a lot of beating. Do the 3rd teams at Sale, Liverpool, Waterloo or Orrell play Percy Park 3rd away, I wonder?

My only regret is that I never captained the club. I had hoped that I could have retired from international rugby after the 1983 British Lions tour to New Zealand and then have had a final year as captain of the club. Hitherto I did not have enough time to devote to the club to do the job properly. They have been marvellous to me over the years and it would have been an appropriate way to end my career, but life does not always work out exactly as desired.

If I had not lived always in Lancashire and could have found a good reason to spend a year in Wales, what I would have liked more than anything would have been to play a season in top-class club rugby down there. There was never any chance of that happening, but I would have loved to play at lock week in week out for Cardiff or Swansea or Llanelli. It is unquestionably the best club rugby anywhere in the world – not only the toughest physically, but also the highest standard technically, with a superb atmosphere all its own. Individual players must improve when they are surrounded by top-class players competing against outstanding teams every week. Very few English sides can compete on an equal footing with the top Welsh clubs. The tragedy of club rugby in most parts of England is that the teams carry too many moderate players and there is very little at stake most Saturdays. The French have a similar structure to the Welsh. It is little wonder that these two countries have tended to dominate the Five Nations Championship in recent years.

The John Player Cup is the nearest we come in England to top competitive rugby and I'm afraid Fylde have never been in any great danger of winning the cup. It would not take too long to give a résumé of our cup run in any particular season, though we did once reach the quarter final in 1977. We beat Solihull after first breaking their spirit. They had to travel three times to Fylde to play that match. The first game was cancelled at lunchtime because of frost; the second journey proved equally fruitless when a blanket of fog descended just before the kick-off. They were unable to build themselves up a third time and we managed to beat them. We then defeated the Gordon League from Gloucester, before losing to Saracens.

More often than not, we seemed to draw clubs like Gosforth or Coventry away early in the competition and that tended to end our interest rather abruptly. Not that we didn't win the odd game against the very top clubs: in my time we've beaten Gosforth, Moseley and Coventry, and the game I remember with the greatest satisfaction and affection was our mammoth victory over Gloucester by 33 points to 3 in 1976. The Gloucester team included all their top players such as Mickey Burton, John Watkins, Peter Butler and Peter Kingston, and we were not in the habit of reducing famous teams like that to tatters as we did that day. Not only was it the best performance from a Fylde side during the seventies, it was certainly the best game I ever played for the club. Coincidentally, it was the first time Hilary watched me play.

At the start of that season one of our club officials held a barbecue and one of the other players brought Hilary along to it. I noticed her early in the evening and managed to spend some time chatting to her, but by the end of the night I was discussing rugby with a few of the lads and did not really expect to see her again. However, a fortnight later, her brother-in-law came to stay for the weekend and asked her if she wanted to watch Gloucester play Fylde. She trooped along with him and as the teams ran onto the field, remarked that she knew the creature in the head band in the Fylde No. 4 jersey. The brother-in-law was half impressed because I had played three times for England by then, but Hilary said I had never mentioned anything about that and anyway she did not appreciate that I was much good. By the end she concluded I was a pretty boring sort of player as she never saw me pass, catch or kick the ball, sell a dummy or do anything in the least bit spectacular. She knew little about rugby at that time, especially forward play.

We met in the club house afterwards and I tried as modestly as possible to point out that it was no great surprise to us to stick 30 points on Gloucester, although, of course, I knew it was the sort of result we might actually expect once or twice every hundred years. We got on very well that evening and that was the start of a beautiful relationship that has lasted ever since. It has been just as well that Hilary has grown to like rugby because virtually all our courting was done travelling to rugby matches, in the bar after the games and mid-week at the Fylde club house after training sessions.

Hilary was willingly conscripted by the Fylde Tea Ladies Committee and a great chunk of our social life still revolves around the club. Whenever an offer came from a rival club trying to tempt me to cross the great divide, Hilary always encouraged me to stay with Fylde and I have no regrets at all that I remained with the one club all my playing days.

I can look back now on my years at Fylde with a great deal of pleasure. If we were not the greatest rugby team in England, we had an enviable reputation for being one of the most hospitable – on and off the pitch! Perhaps the playing standard left a little to be desired, but our record remains as good as most of the other clubs in our corner of England. I would definitely not have wanted to swap my long association with Fylde for any other club in the north. The argument that playing for Fylde held back my career is nonsense. I earned my selection for England through my performances with Lancashire and not with Fylde and that is why it became so important to me to win a place in the Lancashire side.

4

Lancashire

After only one season as an established first-team player at Fylde, I played my first county game for Lancashire, although it was not until the following season that I became a regular member of the county side. I was extremely fortunate to be involved for so many years with such a remarkably well-organized county and it would be difficult to overstate the huge influence Lancashire had on the formative stages of my career.

The county was almost indecently endowed with riches on the playing, coaching and administrative sides, and it was a fantastic feeling for me to rub shoulders with great players like Fran Cotton and Tony Neary at my first squad training session. In 1972 we were also particularly lucky to have one of the game's outstanding coaches in charge – John Burgess. It was a revelation for me to play in a team where everyone knew what their special role was and where everyone actually had the capability to fulfil that role. As coach, John Burgess provided an incredible amount of organization, technical skill, motivation and inspiration, and I admired him enormously for dragging Lancashire back to the top of the tree after a lean spell in the sixties. He laid the foundations for the golden years which Lancashire enjoyed in the seventies and was a terrific influence, not only on me, but on every player who was fortunate enough to pass through his hands. John was, is and always will be a rugby fanatic. We were also blessed with a tremendously enthusiastic and loyal band of supporters who followed us round the country and shared in our many triumphs.

They were part of the marvellous spirit that has recently characterized the play of Lancashire. Under Burgess, the team tried to play a bold brand of running rugby based on a fiercely competitive pack and some brilliant individuals behind the scrum. It has been entertaining and exhilarating rugby and it has been much appreciated by both the players and the spectators. After the 1967 All Blacks tour to Britain, John decided that this was the style of play he wished to adopt for the future. This approach was continued and expanded under the inspired coaching of Des Seabrook when he succeeded John in 1977.

At my first Lancashire session I met a player who was to have a profound influence on my philosophy of the sport. Richard Trickey played over a hundred games for Lancashire and a lot of inferior lock forwards have won caps for England. He was the fittest player I ever came across; I found it very hard to credit the masochistic training schedule he eagerly undertook every season in order to perform like a bionic man on the field of action. He really was perpetual motion. He persuaded me right from the outset that if I wanted to progress I would have to be much fitter than I was. He helped me sort out my priorities and I realized that the ability to time my jump and catch at the line-out was actually only a small part of my overall job as a lock forward. I had also to be fit, strong, fast, and perceptive enough to scrummage, ruck, maul, tackle, cover and support flat out for eighty minutes.

Richard was a permanent fixture in the Lancashire team when I took my first tentative steps towards making the grade at county level. As he always packed down on the right-hand side of the scrum, it didn't take me long to work out that I would have to pack down on the left-hand side. I was not accustomed to this scrummaging position, but I would have gladly played hooker if it meant playing for Lancashire, so I made light of the temporary inconvenience to which this change of position had subjected me.

Three years after Richard dropped out of the Lancashire side he was recalled for a couple of games in 1980. Even though I had established squatters' rights as the right lock in the scrums, a position I had held for several years for England and that summer for the British Lions, he made it abundantly clear to me at the first scrum that whenever we had played together down through the years, he had always been on the right and I had been on the left. He suggested that perhaps it would be tempting fate to change a successful combination at this late stage and, bewildered with his logic, I obediently moved over to the left to accommodate him.

Our first match together was in 1972 at Fylde against Cumberland and Westmorland just three days after the North West Counties had beaten the All Blacks at Workington. I was especially pleased to play my first game for Lancashire on my own home ground among familiar surroundings. I remember being amazed when a fellow came round dishing out free jerseys and socks before the match. As I unwrapped my jersey and put it on, I felt thrilled and terribly proud; even if I achieved nothing else in the next ten years, every time I appeared in our club programme there would be a little asterisk against my name because I was a county player. The game was played at a furious pace and seemed to be over almost before it began, but I did quite well at the line-out and we won 13–nil. However, afterwards I appreciated why Richard Trickey felt the compulsion to be so fit: he played a crucial role on the loose, whereas by the time I arrived at the breakdown, prepared to die for queen, country and John Burgess, the ball was already winging its way out to one of the fly halves.

That was the only county game I played that season, but I was determined to win a regular place in 1973. I was aware how difficult this would be with established players like Richard Trickey and Mike Leadbetter as the men in possession, but to my delight and astonishment

I was selected with Trickey for the first game against Durham. In retrospect, I think I was lucky to be picked so early in my career; the selectors should have played Mike Leadbetter that season, but Mike accepted that his county days were probably over and he was the first person to congratulate me and wish me luck. The following year he turned to Rugby League.

My last away trip to that neck of the woods was the bean feast at Percy Park three years earlier, but I had come a long way since then, and now we travelled up the day before and spent the Friday night at a hotel in Durham. I shared a room with Richard Trickey and that was an unforgettable experience. The first thing he did was to turn off the central heating, open all the windows, and announce there was nothing worse than a stuffy hotel room. Who was I to argue, although I thought I was going to freeze to death? We went down to dinner and he proceeded to gorge his way through half a dozen monster courses before dragging me off to a little pub in a quiet side street where we knocked back a few pints of beer between us.

We returned to the hotel feeling suitably relaxed and I was ready for bed and a good night's sleep. Wrong again. Richard ordered a mountain of sandwiches which he demolished during the next couple of hours while watching the midnight movie on television. I managed to slot in a few hours' sleep before he woke me up at the crack of dawn to drag me down to the restaurant for a huge cooked breakfast.

After breakfast he put on his old brown duffle coat, which had seen a fair bit of service in the cause of rugby, and took me off on a brisk walk to Durham Cathedral. We climbed to the top of the spire to witness the magnificent panoramic view and then went for a long walk in the grounds. He had carried out this ritual every time he played in Durham and for the next eight years I did likewise. It was exhilarating and refreshing. By eleven o'clock, however, Richard's stomach began rumbling ominously and we rushed back to the hotel so that he could consume even more food. To be fair, between us we ate exactly the amount two fifteen-stone rugby players with healthy appetites would be expected to eat. The fact was, though, that I ate absolutely nothing and he went right through the menu. I was rather surprised at half time during the match that he was prepared to make do with a piece of orange. Anyway, enough of the eating habits of the Trickey beast – he was one helluva player and I learned a lot playing alongside him.

His advice before that match was forthright and sound. 'Whatever you do, don't try anything fancy. No side stepping or selling dummies or trying to drop a goal – just stick your head up the prop's backside and shove like a lunatic and contest every blasted line-out no matter where the ball is meant to be thrown. We've plenty of prima donnas in the backs to provide the tricks as long as we provide the ball. Just remember, you are a donkey and behave like one.'

We won that game narrowly with a controversial try right at the end and, to my great relief, I stayed in the side for the next match. Our game against Yorkshire should not have taken place because the pitch at Fylde was frozen, but John Burgess assured us this was in our favour. He claimed the Yorkies didn't want to play on concrete and were desperate to have the game postponed. He said we all knew how soft they were; we could go out and tear them apart. Yorkshire obviously failed to receive a copy of the script because they swarmed all over us in the first ten minutes and rattled up 13 points in double quick time to put us on the rack. After recovering from the initial shock, we clawed our way into contention and stole the match with a score on the final whistle. It had been a hard, bruising battle. The annual Roses game was certainly a match apart and a very special one at that. No matter which county was having the better season, a Roses match was always unpredictable. The battle was so fierce and desperate that it was usually a close, tense affair.

I was injured just before the final in the County Championship when Lancashire lost to Gloucestershire, but I recovered in time to be selected for Lancashire's tour to Rhodesia and South Africa. I was then faced with a difficult dilemma. My sister Alison announced she was going to be married and she expected me to be an usher at the wedding. I explained to her that I had been picked to tour South Africa with Lancashire and would be away; I wasn't sure what to do as I felt I might never be picked again for an overseas tour. Little did I guess then what lay in store for me in the future! In the end I asked her to decide and she said that it was only fair that I should go on the tour.

It was on that tour that I first encountered a young student from Liverpool University who was to play with me for England in the British Lions, Maurice Colclough. He looked a real sight for sore eyes. He had long, bright red, shoulder-length hair and he proved to be a bit of a tearaway. My lasting memory of him on that trip was in Bulawayo for the second game of the tour. After a heavy night out, he took a glucose drink before the game to give him enough energy to survive the eighty minutes, but it was not a wise manoeuvre. Early in the match he made a startling break down the middle of the field from deep in his own half, only to be unceremoniously dumped on the ground just inside enemy territory. At that moment he proceeded to be violently sick. I'm afraid to report that Maurice didn't really feature again on the tour – at least, not on the field of play.

We had a great trip that summer and returned to England to reach the semifinals of the County Championship in 1975 and 1976 before losing to Eastern Counties and Gloucestershire respectively. My disappointment at these defeats was tempered by the fact that we won the title three times in the next five years. We beat Middlesex in 1977, Gloucestershire in 1980 and the North Midlands in my final game of rugby in 1982. I had many of my happiest moments playing for Lancashire and made some of my closest friends. Fran Cotton and Tony Neary were seasoned internationals when I first sneaked into the team, but they were an invaluable source of help and encouragement right from the start and were to become tremendous mates.

Although many of the Lancashire team were England internationals, they never regarded playing for the county as anything except a rare honour and privilege; no player in my time ever downgraded the importance of a game for Lancashire. This all helped forge the phenomenal spirit in the side which is seemingly peculiar to teams in the north and in the south west. By all accounts, an international player representing his county in the south does not share such feelings of utter commitment and involvement, and this is sad for the game. Not that the south produces many England players nowadays. Perhaps their indifferent attitude to the County Championship is partly to blame. Certainly, for me, playing for Lancashire was of paramount importance and everyone shared that deep sense of identity. It was like playing for a club side.

Our recent record for producing internationals compares favourably with any part of England and is similar to the great provincial strength of rugby in New Zealand and South Africa. In those countries, the national selectors concentrate on the big provincial matches; it is rare for someone to win a cap after a series of outstanding performances simply for his club side.

Lancashire can also boast of some unique magic potion for producing captains. In the past seven years the last five England captains have all come from Lancashire – Roger Uttley, Fran Cotton, Tony Neary, myself and Steve Smith. That is surely a great tribute to the whole set-up in Lancashire.

I can look back on a host of epic games for Lancashire, but perhaps two or three stand out for special reasons. In the semifinal of the County Championship in 1977 we played against Gloucestershire when their formidable pack was at its considerable best. That match was at Vale of Lune. On the large hill overlooking the picturesque grounds nestling in the valley, one could see from time to time an enormous pig which spent most of his life on the other side of the hill but which occasionally came up for air to see what all the noise and commotion was on the day of the big game. As our team arrived, one of our front-row forwards remarked when he saw this colossal side of bacon silhouetted against the skyline that one of the Gloucestershire props was out warming up a bit early. I'm sure Mike Burton would not have been too offended if he had been within earshot – probably quite flattered.

At the end of a titanic struggle we edged home by 19 points to 15 with the help of five penalties from our fullback, Dave Gullick. Four days before the final against Middlesex at Blundellsands, Hilary and I were married. My hectic playing schedule had virtually ruled out the possibility of a Saturday wedding as after Christmas we were still in the John Player Cup, with the final of the County Championship and four internationals to be played, and a Lions tour looming up at the end of the season. We got married on the Tuesday and had a fantastic honeymoon: I went training with Lancashire on the Wednesday and with Fylde on the Thursday, but as a special concession I was given permission to spend Friday night at home instead of with the team at their hotel. It didn't seem to do me any harm and we won the final very comfortably indeed to round off an eventful week.

Hilary and her father Ken spent the next three weeks feverishly doing up our new house, which pleased me as I am not what is generally regarded as the natural embodiment of a Do-It-Yourself handyman. Quite the reverse. Hilary refers to me as Frank Spencer, actor Michael Crawford's super-clumsy character, whenever I attack any little job around the house. Everyone acknowledged that I was pretty hopeless in the role of odd-job man, so Hilary arranged for her uncle to put up some wooden shelves in the lounge. The family then wondered if there was any possibility of me taking a large can of wood dye and a paint brush and staining all the wood the same rich brown colour.

'Ho, ho,' quoth I, 'I should think I could just about manage that little trick without a safety net or feeling the need to have a couple of fire engines standing by in case of emergency.' My parents, uncle and Hilary went off for a walk while I proceeded to prove what a cool, calm and totally incompetent handyman I was. I poured the wood dye into a large polystyrene bowl and set to in the lounge. No sooner had the first few master strokes been applied, than I noticed the bottom of the bowl was bubbling away furiously. I don't pretend to understand what the chemical reaction was between the ingredients of the wood dye and the polystyrene, but it frothed all over the carpet. Hastily, I grabbed the bowl and ran through to the kitchen to empty the contents into the brand new kitchen bin, which then proceeded to melt before my very eyes. Apart from ruining the bowl, neatly staining the carpet in the lounge, the kitchen floor and the bin, very little damage was done. I thought the fuss afterwards was out of proportion, but it was an incident that is not easily forgotten. I'm a great believer in the old saying that every cloud has a silver lining and am pleased to report that nowadays I'm not requested or required to do anything in the house. There must be a moral there somewhere.

Hilary enjoyed coming to watch Lancashire play because the team had developed a phenomenally happy family atmosphere; the wives and girlfriends would all go off together for lunch and have a few drinks while we prepared for the game. Our die-hard supporters, and we had thousands, used to travel to away games by car, train, minibus and coach. It was because of the intensity of their support and their very high expectations that we were under pressure to produce our best every time we represented Lancashire. It didn't matter whether someone was playing his first or his sixty-first game for the county, he still felt the same tingling excitement, loyalty and sense of anticipation and apprehension in the changing room before the match. It was really like playing for a club side. If John Burgess was the catalyst behind our triumphs in the early part of the seventies, his successor as coach, Des Seabrook, deserves the credit in recent years. Playing regularly for Lancashire enabled me to bridge the gap between club and international rugby and that is what, tragically, is missing elsewhere in the country. At most, only half a dozen club sides in England would have any chance of surviving if they played in Welsh club rugby every week. Many players in England desperately need to play a batch of matches for Lancashire or the equivalent to have a realistic hope of bridging the enormous chasm between club rugby and playing for England. There is only a handful of county sides that bear the remotest comparison with Lancashire and that is the current plight of the game in England.

I shall return to this theme later, but I am grateful to Lancashire for developing my basic skills and giving me an insight and a vision into the game which has allowed me to make the maximum use of whatever talent I had.

Gloucestershire have had a similar beneficial effect on their players and I reckon the best county match in which I ever participated was the final in 1980 when Lancashire beat Gloucestershire by 21 points to 15. On a wet, muddy, dirty day we scored four tries to one and played some delightful running rugby despite the dreadful conditions. It poured all through the match and people on the banking at Vale of Lune began slithering around up to their ankles in mud. A crowd of 10,000 had turned up. The awful weather and playing surface seemed ideal for the bigger, heavier Gloucestershire pack.

Spurred on by our legion of followers, we fought tooth and nail to contain the Gloucestershire juggernaut and launched some penetrating counterattacks from hairy situations with anything but quality possession. It worked out well for us and we played some breathtaking rugby. The Irish international fullback, Kevin O'Brien, joined in every attack and was suitably rewarded for his efforts with two smashing tries. The pack drove forward to spearhead a movement which produced a try in the right-hand corner for John Carleton, and our other British Lions wing, Mike Slemen, cashed in on a mistake by the opposition to score in the left-hand corner.

In the past few seasons the Lancashire team has usually included nine or ten international players when at full strength, so it is not surprising we have been quite successful. We had five caps in the backs – Kevin O'Brien, John Carleton, Tony Bond, Mike Slemen and Steve Smith. Up front, we had Tony Neary, who was the best open-side flanker I've ever played with or against, Fran Cotton, the only prop in the world who was international class on either the loose or the tight head, Colin Fisher at hooker, and Jim Sydall at lock. Jim thoroughly deserved to win his first cap when I dropped out of the Irish match in 1982.

We also had an exuberant chairman of selectors in former England captain Eric Evans, who used to put a little added pressure on us before each game. His parting shot in the dressing room was always the same. 'Don't forget, lads,' he would say with a big, infectious smile, 'you have the best chairman of selectors in the country, the best set of county selectors in the country, the best coach and committee in the country. We've done our bit, now it's up to you.'

Obviously, I never wanted to end my career by being forced to retire on medical grounds, but there is no doubt in my mind that, that being the case, there could have been no more appropriate finale than to play my very last game of rugby for Lancashire. It was a pleasant bonus that that game should be the one in which Lancashire won the County Championship for the twelfth time in our centenary year.

5

My First Cap – 1975

In the summer of 1974, I embarked on my first overseas tour when I went with Lancashire to South Africa and Rhodesia. The British Lions were also in South Africa that summer and we played some of the same teams as the Lions during our month there. This meant that I was jumping against some of the locks who had played with a reasonable degree of success against the Lions, and as I won a fair amount of line-out ball on that trip, I realized that I was not out of my league in this distinguished company. The tour wetted my appetite for the big league and, for the first time, I appreciated that I did have the necessary driving ambition to reach for the top. I was quite conscious that I might never make the grade at the highest level but, at least, I returned home to Lancashire determined to have a go.

At the start of the new season Tonga came to England on tour and I was selected to play against them for the North of England at Birkenhead Park on the Tuesday prior to the England Under-23 game against them on the following Saturday at Twickenham, for which I had been chosen as a travelling reserve. The Tongans, like so many of the rugby teams from the Pacific Islands, were marvellous runners and handlers, but they were not particularly noted for their line-out technique and I had a decent game as the North of England beat them quite convincingly. To prepare and play in that match meant I had to take Monday and Tuesday off work in the family textile business. As I was only a reserve on the Saturday for the Under-23 team, I phoned the RFU at Twickenham to ask if it would be all right for me to join the team on Friday; I explained I did not want to take time off work on Thursday and Friday.

I was told that that would be in order but apparently the team had expected me to pitch up for training on the Friday afternoon. I arrived at the hotel late in the evening to be informed that as I had missed the line-out practice on the previous two days, they would hold an impromptu session especially for me in the hotel car park on the Saturday morning. Peter Colston, the England Under-23 coach, duly dragged me out of bed, and John Raphael, the hooker and captain, threw the ball at me for a quarter of an hour and then went over all the line-out signals in case I came on during the match. I was naive in those days and never bothered to take a track suit with me, so I practised in the car park in my jeans and a sweater and borrowed a track suit for the match in the afternoon when I was sitting on the bench.

After lunch we set off for the ground and I entered Twickenham for the first time. I was fascinated by the immense size of the changing room, the shining polished floor, and how remarkably clean and tidy everything was. All the jerseys were hung up round the room beginning with No. 1 and continuing in a clockwise direction. Most rugby changing rooms are stuffy, cramped, scruffy places and I had never witnessed anything resembling the palatial luxury of Twickenham. Instead of the usual large communal bath generally favoured by rugby clubs, there were lots of old-fashioned, individual cast-iron baths. For me it was a new, exciting and different world and I was lucky enough to justify a bath by the end of the afternoon.

Ensconced in my borrowed track suit, I sat with the other substitutes watching the match in the knowledge that I was unlikely to get on as I was only acting as cover for two lock forwards. Mal Malik, the Coventry flanker, was replacement for the back row and he must have felt the adrenaline flowing when our No. 8, Trevor

Cheeseman, was concussed just after half time. However, a brief discussion among the selectors resulted in my being sent on to play at lock and Neil Mantell being switched from lock to No. 8. Just before four o'clock on a dull, overcast day, I sprinted onto the Twickenham pitch for the first time in an England jersey to represent my country, albeit at Under-23 level.

It was a thrilling experience even though the crowd was only two or three thousand and I thoroughly enjoyed the match. We were leading comfortably at the time and it is easy to come on as a replacement in such circumstances and mingle with all the other donkeys for a few minutes while settling in. Needless to say, the morning line-out practice in the hotel car park had been wasted on me. I had forgotten all the signals and all the calls in my excitement, but Steve Smith, at scrum half, looked after me and at least told me when to expect the ball on our own throw-in. I did quite well at the line-out and was reasonably conspicuous in the loose. Having achieved my biggest honour to date, I felt thrilled at the thought that that I just might, one day, return to Twickenham to play in a full international.

In those days of organized chaos, the England selectors ran a complicated series of trials which were specifically designed to confuse everyone, but they also provided me with my next opportunity to scramble one more rung up the ladder towards my first cap. I was picked alongside Roger Uttley at lock for the North of England against the Midlands at Headingley and we were to play against Nigel Horton and a Coventry lock called Derek Simpson. Roger jumped at 2 and Horton at 4 for England, which meant that I would inevitably be expected to spend the afternoon jumping against Horton in the middle of the line. I appreciated my career was hardly likely to prosper from this particular experience as I would have precious little chance of winning any ball against Horton.

I could scarcely believe my good fortune when we arrived for training on the Friday evening. Our captain,

Fran Cotton, asked Roger if he would mind taking on Nigel Horton in the middle of the line to allow me an opportunity to advance my cause. Roger was a firmly established player and was guaranteed a place in the final trial, but I must have posed some tiny threat to him as a potential England front jumper. A large percentage of players would have insisted on playing in their best position, but to my amazement and delight, Roger willingly agreed to the switch. I remain greatly indebted to Fran and Roger for this extremely generous act. To have been cleaned out by Horton could have resulted in my instant return to relative obscurity and would have seriously retarded my progress.

As it transpired, we won the match comfortably by 28 points to 13 and I had one of my better games. Our team were much more organized and disciplined than the Midlands, which helped Roger Uttley play well too. After the match I had to dash straight back to Fylde to a party that evening and as it was only a fortnight before Christmas, I bade everyone farewell, wishing them the compliments of the season and saying I would see them in the New Year. Fran told me that, in fact, I would see everyone the following Saturday at Twickenham for the final trial. I didn't really believe for a second I would make the trial, but I left in good heart in the knowledge that I just might be on the near periphery of the England squad of thirty.

On the Monday morning my colleague and fellow trialist at Fylde, wing threequarter Tony Richards, phoned me up to tell me that the press had been in touch with him to say we had both been selected for the minnow side in the final trial. A good game now would establish me in the squad; give or take a few injuries or a flu epidemic, I could soon be in the England team.

The trial posed a few interesting problems. At the front of the line-out I was up against Roger Uttley and I was just sharp enough to work out for myself that he might be marginally less cooperative in this match than he had been the previous week.

Following the usual disastrous number of withdrawals from the two teams in the seventy-two hours preceding the trial, it was a mixed bag of thirty players that eventually assembled on the Saturday afternoon. Originally, the Rest locks were Nigel Horton and I, against Roger Uttley and Chris Ralston, but Chris withdrew, Horton was promoted and Bob Wilkinson became my new partner. We were both vastly inexperienced for such a confrontation and I had a rough idea how the Christians must have felt being thrown to the lions. My sagging confidence and the general feeling of hopelessness one experiences when fighting an apparently lost cause was given a terrific boost when I shuffled into the changing room. Our captain, Dave Rollitt, came over and addressed me with: 'And just who the hell are you, may I ask?' It was scarcely the red-carpet treatment and I stood there feeling thoroughly inadequate. Not only had he never seen me play rugby, but, seemingly, he had never even heard of me. However, as an afterthought, he did give me a hint of encouragement when he added, 'I suppose if you have been selected for an England trial you can't be completely useless. You presumably know you're meant to jump at the line-out and push in the scrums.'

It is a grim reflection on the desperate organization of those days in the mid seventies that we only met half an hour before the kick-off, had to be introduced to each other and had no time to sort out all the various signals for all the different pieces of set play. Consequently, and not surprisingly, the line-out play, and, of course, the trial, was a bit of a disaster. I was able to crack our opponents' line-out signals before I could fathom out our own and it was well nigh impossible to build up any sort of understanding with our hooker, John Pullin, about the way I liked the ball thrown in in this, our first match together.

The senior side in the trial had previously played together a fair amount and with this distinct advantage they gave us a real thumping by 38 points to 22, including eight tries to three. Naturally, I was disappointed at losing. However, I had not been completely outplayed at the line-out and had popped up every so often to make a contribution in the loose, so I gleaned some satisfaction from my own performance in difficult circumstances.

We all went our different ways over Christmas while we waited for news of the team to play against Ireland. The best present Santa Claus could possibly have brought me that Christmas was the announcement that I had been included in the squad of thirty for a special weekend training session before the Irish match.

My initial reaction was one of immense relief and great excitement, but I was soon to receive a severe body blow. For the previous couple of months both Tony Richards and I had, with an unashamed air of covetousness, been under the firm impression that once we were in the full England squad for the Home Championship, a whole selection of goodies would be offloaded in our direction. On the way down to London for the squad session we discussed how, apart from a pair of boots and a smart Adidas hold-all, we would be given an official England track suit with the rose there for all to see. We talked about how, if we achieved nothing else in the rest of our careers (and that was a distinct possibility), we would always be able to run around in an England track suit. Well, we were soon to find out just how old Mother Hubbard felt when she opened her cupboard to discover it was bare.

We received nothing at all that weekend. Not only did we both feel dejected and depressed that our achievements fell below the bottom line of such significant recognition, we also half froze to death as we had, in our youthful zest and optimism, neglected to take our Fylde track suits with us. It may sound rather petty and trivial, but when, a fortnight later, I did receive my England track suit as a reserve for the Irish game, it was one of the happiest moments of my life. I felt a tremendous surge of pride when I put it on and, for the first few weeks, I must confess that I wore it rather a lot although I did not go quite so far as to sleep in it.

That squad session ended on Sunday at lunchtime and I stayed down in London because I had some business to do at Olympia on the Monday. There was a big camping exhibition on there and my uncle Joseph and I had an order for an enormous amount of canvas. That evening as we were walking from the tube station to the hotel, I asked my uncle to give me a couple of minutes to buy a paper to see who was in the England team. I knew there was no possibility of my being in the team because Roger Uttley was certain to be the front jumper. It seemed extremely unlikely that I would be one of the six reserves but I was more than a little curious to see who in fact had been selected. There, on the back page of the *Evening Standard*, I saw the England team in big, bold type and, in smaller print underneath, the names of the six substitutes. My name was the last of the six in the list and I stood there shaking with excitement, reading it over and over again to make sure it was not a mistake. I showed it to my uncle, phoned my parents at home and then, after the reality had sunk in, we went out on the town to celebrate with a few beers.

Although there is an unwritten rule that a player calls off from his club side the Saturday before his very first international in case he is injured, I played for Fylde against Nuneaton because I was only a replacement for the match in Dublin the following week. After the Nuneaton match was over I went into the club house where I was met by our club secretary, Arthur Bell, and one of the England selectors, John Elders. They were deep in conversation and looking very concerned about a letter which Arthur was holding. He showed me the letter, which had been sent to the club but was specifically for my attention. It was from the IRA and warned me not to travel to Dublin for the international or I would be risking serious repercussions. I looked at Arthur and John and said that I had just received the biggest honour of my life and it was going to take far more than a threatening letter from the IRA to stop me turning up at Lansdowne Road to sit on the England bench for the first time in my career. I pointed out that it might be the nearest I would ever get to an England cap; not wild horses and certainly not the IRA were going to stop me. It was decided that the letter should be handed over to the police and after discussion with them and John Elders, it was agreed that I should take my place in the England party.

When I turned up for training with the rest of the squad on the Thursday afternoon in London at the Stoop Memorial Ground, one of the England props, Robin Cowling, came over and told me that I might be in the team. I couldn't believe that my incredible run of good luck could possibly continue unabated, but I asked him what the story was. He said that on the train coming down to London Roger Uttley had knackered his back bending over to pick up a piece of apple pie. I can just imagine telling people in thirty years' time when they ask me how I won my first cap for England that there was this great England and British Lions lock forward called Roger Uttley who tried to lift up a piece of apple pie from his plate and his back seized up, so I was called into the team. It may sound a bit far-fetched but that is more or less what happened. I took his place throughout the training session on Thursday but by the evening there was still no official announcement about who would play lock alongside Chris Ralston on the Saturday. I felt the selectors would probably send out an SOS for Nigel Horton as he was far more experienced than I was, but I went off to bed early knowing that it was not entirely outside the bounds of possibility that the former fly half of Cressbrook School Under-10s could become lock forward for England.

At seven o'clock on the Friday morning, Alec Lewis, the chairman of selectors, came to my bedroom, woke me up, shook me warmly by the hand and said, 'Congratulations, you are in the team tomorrow to play Ireland – good luck.' I was in. I had really made it. Dame

Fortune unquestionably had a soft spot for me and, at the relatively tender age, for a lock forward, of twenty-three, I was about to experience the greatest thrill in the world of representing my country on the rugby field.

We flew to Dublin that afternoon and for security reasons both the England and the Irish teams were booked into the Shelbourne Hotel. After dinner the boys rustled up a card school and I managed to hit a winning streak. At the end of a couple of hours, I had given my bank balance a healthy boost of around £50 and I reckoned that life wasn't too bad really. I was sharing a room with Chris Ralston and after watching the late film on television, was ready for a good night's sleep. Chris asked if I minded if he smoked a cigar and my last memory before falling asleep was of seeing the red glow of his cigar in the dark, the whiff of tobacco and the sound of coughing. I woke up at first light on the Saturday morning with a similar attack on the same senses. I could see the red glow on the end of Chris's first cigar of the new day – at least I think it was his first – smell the stale stench of tobacco and hear the coughing. Rumour had it that Chris used to disappear into the showers immediately before a match to steal a few puffs on the weed before running onto the field. Be that as it may, he was a superb forward and I was extremely fortunate to have him there to take the pressure off me.

I made a half-hearted assault on the fare at breakfast but didn't really do it justice. With my mind on other things, I skipped lunch altogether and spent the morning in my room skimming over the papers to see if any of the scribblers thought I had deserved my promotion and taking phone calls from my family.

The first cap is a very special occasion and it remains a regret to me that my family were not really able to share it properly with me. They had sensibly decided not to spend a small fortune on air tickets and hotels to watch me sit in my new maroon track suit in the stand all afternoon. By the time I had been drafted into the team it was too late to make any arrangements. All my family, friends and relations phoned to wish me luck. Then, after a team talk from our new coach, John Burgess, we set off with a police escort to the match.

When we arrived at the ground there were sixty or so telegrams waiting on the table in our changing room. Fifty of these were for me and after I had opened a few, John Burgess told me to put them all away until after the match. We had arrived an hour before the kick-off and after I'd changed into my kit, I spent about half an hour in the loo. I was incredibly nervous and excited, my mind trying to cope with a whole gamut of emotions. My mind was also trying to prepare the ground for the forthcoming confrontation of the first line-out with Ireland's front jumper. He was a man called Willie John McBride, whose fearsome reputation stretched to every corner of the world. He had already played fifty-nine times for Ireland, been on five British Lions tours – a record – and had just returned from captaining the unbeaten Lions in South Africa. It struck me that it was just conceivable he might not be completely overawed at the prospect of the imminent conflict with W. B. Beaumont of Fylde – potential one-cap wonder. On the other hand, I was trembling from the top of my head to the end of my big toe and the main memory I have of before the game was standing on my tiptoes in the team photograph in the hope that I would look almost as tall as Chris Ralston. I used to have a superstition about running out of the tunnel and onto the pitch last, a superstition which just happened to be shared by David Duckham. After the final rousing call to arms by our captain, Fran Cotton, every player came over to shake my hand and wish me luck, and Duckham said that I could run out onto the pitch last of all.

I could hardly believe the roar which greeted us as we ran on – it was a bit different from Fylde every week or Preston Grasshoppers – but it was nothing compared to the tremendous crescendo of noise that heralded the appearance of the Irish side led by the great Willie John

McBride. This was the first opportunity the Irish had had to express their feelings for Willie John since he had returned triumphant from the 1974 Lions tour and the applause was deafening.

Eventually the game kicked off and soon we had the first line-out. For the previous five years Willie John had been my idol and I had hoped that one day I would be the same type of player and, perhaps, with a generous slice of luck, I might enjoy just a taste of the sort of respect and success he had always commanded. At the first line-out I turned to look at him and I remember the disdain and almost contempt with which he glared at me. Before the match Fran had assured me he was an old man, well past his peak, and he couldn't jump at the best of times, but I soon realized that the King was not yet dead – he had no intention of being dethroned by me that afternoon. He leaned all over me to win that first line-out and Fran immediately shouted at me not to let McBride dictate the course of events or I would be quickly overwhelmed. He told me to roll up my sleeves, get stuck in and have a go. Shortly afterwards, Ireland were on the attack and they threw to Willie John at the front. I thundered forward and with one hand tapped it down to Jan Webster, who cleared it to touch. The psychological barrier was broken and I settled down determined to contest every ball with every ounce of strength I could muster. Oddly enough, the ball was rarely thrown to the front during the rest of the match, but when it was, I gave as good as I got and my particular battle with Willie John ended fairly even.

The speed of the game took me by surprise. The match flashed past in a blur and I was unable to make the sort of forceful contribution in the loose which I did every week at club and county level. Although our pack had the better of the forward exchanges, we lost 12–9. With only ten minutes left we led 9–6 but then we got into an awful muddle at a scrum in front of our post. We heeled, but Rossborough at fullback slipped as Webster passed

Above: (inset)
Happy, smiling
baby. I had just
been told the result
from Cardiff: Wales
3 – England 8, 1953.
Twenty-seven years
later, mission
accomplished: Grand
Slam champions

Right: Less happy in
my new role as
spectator after
thirty-four caps

Remembering my fly-half training for the North of England against Tonga in 1974

Above: Lancashire coach Des Seabrook holding the Thorn EMI Trophy in 1980

Left: In the jersey I wore most – playing for Fylde

Proudly clutching the Thorn EMI trophy, I'm being lifted by Fran Cotton (not for the first time that day!) and Dave Tabern

Leaving the field of play for the very last time

Lancashire – County Champions, 1980: *Back row (left to right):* D. Tabern, R. Creed, T. Morris, T. Simon, K. Pacey, C. Fisher; *Middle row:* D. Seabrook (coach), E. Evans (chairman of selectors), K. Aitchison, D. Carfoot, A. Neary, L. Connor, J. Sydall, F. Cotton, A. Gott (honorary secretary), E. Deasey (team secretary). *Front row:* J. Heaton, P. Philips, M. Sleman, W. B. Beaumont (captain), J. Walsh (president), J. Carleton, A. Wright, P. Williams, S. Smith, K. O'Brien

Above: Support! My colleagues decided I was big enough to look after myself

Below: Geoff Wheel and myself passing the time of day during a lull in the England-Wales match

Losing the third Test to New Zealand was not a bundle of laughs *(right)* ... but scoring tries was, as Peter Wheeler shows *(bottom)*

Below: The best front row in the world in 1977 – Graham Price, Peter Wheeler and Fran Cotton

'Hey, donkeys, you'll never believe what I've just seen' – Steve Smith

Erica Roe shares the spotlight during my half-time team talk. I still managed to make a couple of points – so did she

Unique picture of All Blacks three-man scrum against the Lions in the fourth Test

Above: Steve Smith scores against Ireland in the first match of the Grand Slam season in 1980

Below: John Carleton scores on the way to victory over France in Paris

and the Irish fly half, Billy McCombe, burst through to gather the ball, score by the posts and convert.

At the final whistle I was heartbroken that we had lost a game I thought we should have won – a game I had desperately wanted to win. I slumped down in the changing room and burst into tears. John Burgess comforted me as I mulled over all the hundreds of things I knew I should have done. It came home forcibly to me that winning a cap was not the be-all and end-all. I wanted more than anything else to play for England again and to play in a winning team. I appreciated too that I needed to be fitter to play at this level – I only just arrived at most of the rucks and mauls as the ball popped out. In this determined frame of mind, I reckon I learned a lot from my first game of international rugby.

My only memory of the evening's festivities was at the dinner. When Willie John McBride stood up to speak, he received a magnificent spontaneous standing ovation. He was one of the game's great forwards, great captains and great characters, and he had led both Ireland and the Lions with rare distinction. I was reassured that when, as a rookie teenager, I had put Willie John on a pedestal as my ideal lock forward and dreamed one day of emulating his achievements, I had made a pretty good choice.

6

Down Under on Tour – 1975

The next international was against France at Twickenham two weeks later and I was left out in favour of
Roger Uttley who had recovered from his back injury.
I had fully expected the selectors to make this change
and I was delighted to be named as one of the six
replacements because this meant they must have been
reasonably satisfied with my game against Ireland.
Strangely enough, Roger nearly played the role of my
guardian angel for the second time in a fortnight. Towards the end of the match he received a terrific whack
on the side of his head that split his ear and opened up
a nasty gash which required eighteen stitches. Only a
few minutes of the game remained but the selectors told
me to go down to the tunnel immediately and be ready
to go on. To a rumbling chorus of 'Lucky sod' from the
other substitutes, I made my way down to the pitch with
just one thought racing through my mind – I was not
going to be a 'one-cap wonder'.

When I reached the tunnel though, I saw Leon Walkden, the RFU doctor, furiously taping Roger's head and
was told he would be able to complete the match and I
would not be required. What was much harder to accept
and understand was the fact that I was not required
again that season in any capacity. From almost playing
in my second international, I found myself bombed out
of the squad altogether for the last two matches of the
season. After the defeat by France, I think the selectors
started to panic and in the space of the next month they

changed more than half the team in a bizarre series of illogical moves.

The one which directly affected me was the decision to drop Andy Ripley and replace him at No. 8 with Roger Uttley. They recalled Nigel Horton to partner Chris Ralston in the second row, which meant they had plenty of cover at lock; also they needed a back-row replacement to sit on the bench, not a lock forward. I could understand the decision to recall Horton because he was a hard, experienced forward and I certainly did not begrudge him his selection. In fact, looking back, it strikes me as disgraceful the way the selectors regularly abused two such outstanding players as Horton and Ripley. Both deserved far more caps than they actually won.

We were comprehensively thumped at Cardiff by a very good Welsh team who deservedly went on to win the Championship and the selectors proceeded to put a whole lot of new names into the hat for the final match of the season against Scotland. Nigel Horton, Peter Wheeler, John Watkins and Fran Cotton all disappeared from the pack and the selectors brought in four different backs as well.

Arguably Scotland should have won the Calcutta Cup despite the fact that four of their pack were shielding injuries and played with pain-killing injections. In the last quarter of an hour when they were trailing by 7 points to 6, Dougie Morgan missed two relatively simple kicks at goal which would have given Scotland their first Triple Crown since 1938.

To finish the domestic season with a win was none the less important because England were about to tour Australia that summer and at least the selectors had something, or should have had something, on which to base their team. In fact they proceeded to make an unbelievable mess of picking the touring party, setting English rugby right back. Since the turn of the year, I had hoped to be included in the touring party because there were only four locks in the squad of thirty and with Roger

Uttley able to double up in the back row there seemed every likelihood they would take all four of us.

I was a little concerned when I disappeared from the substitutes' bench after the French international, but I had not blotted my copybook and as no other lock had been introduced in my place, I remained ever hopeful. When the touring party was announced to my great relief I was included, but I must admit I was astounded at the horrific botch the selectors had made over all. For such a demanding and challenging tour, they swept aside a whole range of experienced, seasoned internationals and went overboard to encourage new, raw, untried talent. It seemed a crazy, pointless exercise and, despite the valiant efforts of our coach, John Burgess, it was doomed to failure. Alan Old and Steve Smith were clearly the best halfbacks around but neither were selected at the start of the tour. The total number of caps amongst the four halfbacks who were chosen at the outset of the trip – Wordsworth, Bennett, Ashton and Kingston – came to just one. To try out so much raw youth in such key positions as an experimental exercise in my opinion bordered on lunacy. That season Peter Rossborough and Tony Jorden had each played two internationals and spent the whole year training and practising with the squad. The selectors then rejected both of them and picked two uncapped players in Peter Butler and Alistair Hignell.

I was flabbergasted to see neither Chris Ralston nor Nigel Horton in the party. The short-sighted policy of the selectors had given me a golden opportunity to win two more England caps. Apart from myself and Uttley, Bob Wilkinson and Neil Mantell were the only other two locks in the party and both were uncapped.

The final indictment of the selectors is seen best in the progress made by the plethora of rookies who flew to Australia. The idea that they would learn from the tour and then establish themselves in the England team in the near future was soon blown sky high. Ten of that touring party went on to win a pathetic total of ten caps between them and their contribution to English rugby was minimal. Once one or two of the senior pros like Fran Cotton and Tony Neary were injured, we were, needless to say, in deep trouble.

We began with a huge win over Western Australia in Perth by 64 points to 3, but thereafter the tour became very hard and sometimes unpleasant work. We flew 3000 miles across Australia for the second match and before we had recovered from the journey we lost to Sydney by 14 points to 10. It was not a match I look back on with any degree of affection. Late in the first half I was running across the field following the ball after a line-out when the Sydney prop, Steve Finnane, hammered me to the ground with a pulverizing left hook. I was nowhere near the ball at the time and in no way interfering with Finnane or anyone else when the punch was thrown. It was the sort of mindless act of unprovoked aggression that sickens me in rugby and I have the utmost contempt for the senseless perpetrators of such acts of violence. Finnane had previously laid out a couple of other members of the England team that afternoon, Mike Burton and Steve Callum, and we were unfortunately to encounter him twice more on the tour. When I regained consciousness, Tony Neary insisted that I left the field for treatment and very grudgingly I accepted his advice. Disaster struck again in the second half when Fran Cotton trapped a nerve in his back and played no further part in the tour.

I did not play in our crushing win at Perth and I also missed our 29–24 win over New South Wales in Sydney on the Saturday before the first Test. This meant my only hope of clinching a place in the Test side was to play well in the mid-week match against the New South Wales Country XV and pray for an emphatic victory. Such was the available talent bequeathed us by the folly of the selectors back in England that our mid-week, dirt-tracker team managed to lose 14–13 to the Country XV and I had to resign myself to a seat on the substitutes' bench for the first international in Sydney.

In the first two matches in Sydney we came across a handful of abrasive characters in Finnane, Peter Horton and Ray Price. All three were picked for the Test and it was no surprise that it turned out to be an abrasive, tough, unpleasant game. It was depressing that the Australians were prepared to adopt such tactics in their bid to win at any costs, because they had a good side and in between bursts of naked aggression, they produced some breathtaking rugby. The whole team joined in brilliant waves of running and handling. If they had concentrated their energies on running the ball for eighty minutes instead of trying to intimidate our team, they might well have won much more convincingly than 16–9. I came on midway through the first half to replace Tony Neary, who had injured his ribs, and although I was pleased to collect a second cap, I was disappointed at the spirit in which the game was played. I was marking Reg Smith at the front of the line-out and I did quite well at winning my share of the ball, while in the loose I had my best game of the tour thus far.

On the Tuesday I played alongside Bob Wilkinson at lock in our easy win over Queensland and we were both selected for the second Test in Brisbane. This was, therefore, the first time I had actually been selected for an international as first choice and I was looking forward to the challenge. For my first cap I had come in as a last-minute replacement for Uttley and for my second cap I also came on as a replacement. I thought that nothing could spoil the thrill of winning my third cap strictly on merit. How wrong can a man be?

My own memories of that now infamous match are, of necessity, a trifle vague. The Australian team had been psyched up way beyond the normal levels of acceptability and they began the match like caged wild animals who had been starved for a week. From the kick-off Barry Nelmes fell on the ball and the Aussies proceeded to kick him all over the field. It was as if their coach, Dave Brockoff, had told them to go out and act as if each player was a bull in a china shop. After poor

Nelmes released the ball, it was scrambled into touch and that gave way to the most notorious line-out in modern international rugby. It began before the ball was thrown in with a threatening verbal altercation between Stuart MacDougall, the Australian loose-head prop, and Mike Burton. The ball was thrown in and all hell broke loose. All at once, before I realized what was happening, I was hit by a flurry of punches thrown by several different Australian players, and one right hook exploded on my face to open up a gaping cut above my right eye.

The referee, Bob Burnett, eventually restored some sort of order and I stood there with blood pouring down my face scarcely able to believe the disgraceful, shameful scene that had just taken place. The England captain, John Pullin, looked at me and told me to go off and have the cut stitched but I protested, saying there was no way I was going to leave the field. The referee then ordered me off to receive medical attention and very grudgingly I left. I ran to the changing room where the doctor inserted half a dozen stitches in double quick time. As he was putting some tape round my head for added protection, I heard the clatter of studs reverberating along the concrete corridor. The door was flung open and in came Mike Burton looking thoroughly dejected. I asked him if the sods had nobbled him too, but he didn't reply. As I ran out of the changing room, I asked him if he was all right, but again he made no reply. I assumed he had pulled a hamstring or something and I expected to see the replacement, Phil Blakeway, on the pitch when I returned.

The tour manager, Alec Lewis, was waiting for me on the touch line and he explained that in the third minute of the match Mike, having already been penalized for butting one of the Australians, had been sent off for late tackling the left wing, Osborne. The horror of the situation really sunk in when Alec told me I would have to play prop for the last seventy-five minutes of the match.

My last game at prop had been for Fylde 3rd in 1972

– not the ideal preparation for the ordeal I was now about to endure. I was up against MacDougall and to my delight we only lost one tight head all afternoon and our scrummage remained surprisingly solid throughout. My neck and back were sore for several days afterwards and one of the Australian forwards took the trouble to add to my discomfort early in the second half in a particularly unsavoury incident. Our scrum collapsed and as I lay there trapped on the ground I saw a boot swing in my direction. I closed my eyes and turned my head as far to my left as I could to protect my cut right eye and waited a split second for the impact. Sure enough, the boot connected on the side of my head with an almighty thump but, apart from a splitting headache, inflicted no visible damage.

We only lost by 30 points to 21 although they scored five tries to two, but, inevitably, playing with only fourteen men virtually the whole match, we tired in the last twenty minutes and were finally overrun. At half time we actually led 15–9 – Alan Old kicking three penalties and converting a try by Squires – and with a full team I'm sure we would have won.

The dinner in the evening was tense to say the least. Tempers were frayed on both sides; it had not been a match in which anyone could have been proud to have participated.

I utterly deplore all forms of dirty play and it is sickening to think that premeditated violence should ever occur in rugby union. It is an amateur sport played for fun and enjoyment. It should always be remembered that, come Monday morning, the players all have to go back to work to earn a living and support their families. The first few minutes of that appalling match in Brisbane produced the most wickedly lethal play I have ever known anywhere in the world and the Australians have a lot to answer for. The team was psyched up to the eyeballs and a few of their players were prepared to kick and punch anyone in a white jersey. Obviously, several players, including John Hipwell, their captain, would never resort to such scandalous behaviour, but it struck me at the time that some of their team like Horton and Price seemed only too keen to win at any cost. It would have been better for Australia and the game of rugby if players like these two and Finnane had not been selected and instead had been encouraged to turn their attentions to some other more suitable sport – perhaps head hunting in Borneo or some form of martial arts.

I have had enormous admiration for Australian rugby in recent years. They have produced a host of brilliant backs and some world-class forwards like Mark Loane and Garrick Fay. They have played a great deal of wonderful running rugby and had excellent results against all the top countries at international level. During the past three or four years I have got to know many of the current members of the Australian team and we have got on extremely well, both on and off the field. They have earned and deserved the respect and admiration of rugby players and followers everywhere. But, in emphasizing their marvellous contribution to the development of the game, I feel compelled to point out that one black episode in their history in 1975 and mention the players who tarnished, temporarily at least, their country's tremendous reputation.

Rugby is a hard, tough, physical-contact sport and I hope it will always remain exactly that, but it is only too easy for one player to maim or seriously injure another if he really wants to during a match. For that simple reason there has to be a code of gentlemanly conduct to play the game in the right spirit or the game will not be worth playing at all. I would like to think that I have never started any trouble at any level of the game and I have never, with or without premeditation, ever tried deliberately to maim another player. When, from time to time, a player has taken a swing at me during a match, I have tended to return the compliment. In that respect I am not claiming to be whiter than white, but even in the occasional altercations in which I have been involved, and of which I am not particularly proud, there is a code of ethics to which I have always adhered, and kicking or booting someone on the ground is way outwith that code. It is only by playing in the right spirit that the game will flourish and both players and spectators will derive the fun and the pleasure which is the whole purpose of rugby. If certain people have other, less honourable, objectives, clubs and countries will do rugby union a great service by never selecting them. Players, especially at international level where there is vast media coverage, have an obligation and a duty to set a good example to the school children who watch them and want one day to emulate them. I am depressed by parents telling me they are not sure if they should allow their children to play rugby because it looks so rough and dangerous. Unfortunately, the occasional isolated, unpleasant incident clouds their view. It is up to everyone to help to eliminate those incidents.

Perhaps the most influential individual in this respect is the referee. A lot of the aggression on a rugby pitch is born of frustration when a poor referee allows one side a distinct advantage, usually by ignoring the off-side law or allowing a team to kill the ball in the loose. If a referee fails to keep a tight grip on the game, there lurks a temptation for the players to take the law into their own hands. It is a disturbing fact that in recent years the standard of refereeing, particularly at international level, has dropped alarmingly. I think the best referees in my playing time have all been French. I reckon that Georges Domercq, Jean-Pierre Bonnet and Francis Palmade all shared a real feeling for the game, a perfect interpretation of the advantage law and a complete understanding of the laws and their practical application. They earned the respect of the players and had no trouble in keeping control on the field. These three referees had the right attitude; by exerting their influence on a game they had no need to be whistle-happy and punctilious. They clearly loved rugby and they helped the players to play and enjoy the game in the best possible spirit.

British referees have tended in recent years to blow up for everything and that ruins any hope of a flowing game. The two for whom I have had the highest regard are Clive Norling of Wales and John West of Ireland, who both have this innate feel for the game. Like the best referees, they stand no nonsense. Norman Sanson of Scotland was another outstanding referee, but England has not had a top referee since Johnny Johnson retired in the mid seventies. During my two Lions tours I have had every sympathy for the referees which has not always been reciprocated. In front of their own home crowds, they are under huge pressure to spend the match only looking for the Lions' mistakes, but in South Africa Steve Strydom and in New Zealand Dave Miller both coped admirably in difficult circumstances.

The great thing about rugby, though, is the uncanny willingness of players to accept the referee's decision without a whimper even when it is palpably wrong. They give a salutary lesson to the whole world of professional sport. I could be mistaken but I have a tiny hunch that tennis players such as Ilie Nastase and John McEnroe might have a little difficulty adjusting to rugby's code of sportsmanship. Professional soccer players would be at a similar disadvantage because traditionally they are not well suited temperamentally to the code of conduct which is willingly accepted by rugby players.

In 1981 England could have shared the Championship, but they lost the crucial match against France at Twickenham because of a terrible mistake by the referee, Alan Hosie. England lost in the end by 16 points to 12 but the referee quite wrongly awarded France 6 points. The controversial score came when Marcus Rose, the England fullback, fielded a long speculative kick ahead inside his own 22. He pumped the ball right-footed high into the west stand where it landed in the RFU committee box and was caught by Dickie Jeeps, former England and British Lions scrum half and currently chairman of the Sports Council. Meanwhile, strictly against the laws of the game, the French scrum half Berbizier took a quick throw-in using a completely different ball which he grabbed from a surprised ball boy. France scored the winning try when Rives passed to Lacans and Laporte converted from the touch line. Those 6 points made all the difference to the final result. Hosie should have insisted that the line-out be retaken and the original ball used. However, he awarded the try and not one of our players protested then or afterwards. As captain of the team, I mentioned it to him in passing and he shrugged his shoulders, claiming the ball Rose kicked into the stand was the same one France used to take the quick throw. It patently was not and while the conversion was being taken I raised the subject with Brian Anderson, the touch judge on that side of the field. He pointed out that I was absolutely right but he could only interfere with the match and attract the referee's attention for specified offences such as outbreaks of violence on the field. One of the wags in our team suggested in the bath afterwards that I should have gone over and whacked Hosie; Anderson would then have been in a position to intervene because of the outbreak of violence and sort out the whole question. However, it is typical of the attitude of rugby players that, apart from my half-hearted questioning of Hosie, not a murmur of dissent was heard. Had that been a similar incident in the final of the soccer World Cup between Italy and West Germany, I hate to think what would have happened either on the pitch or amongst the rival groups of spectators on the terraces.

Happily, rugby is played by a civilized section of the community and they are disciplined enough to accept the referee's decisions no matter how wrong he may be. But this only goes to emphasize the need to rid the game once and for all of the tiny, but evil, minority of dirty players who believe they are above the law and can execute any form of carnage they wish on the field of play. There is no place for such animals at any level of the game.

7

The Whitewash of 1976

After the second Test in Brisbane, there had been speculation that the unsavoury behaviour of the Australians in that match might lead to the cancellation of their four-month tour of the British Isles at the start of the 1975–76 season. In the event, the tour went ahead and England's first international against Australia was to be on 3 January 1976.

From the moment the catastrophic selection had been made by England for the tour to Australia, it was inevitable that the trip would be disastrously unsuccessful, and so it transpired. With so many mediocre players in the party, John Burgess had found it impossible to develop the style of rugby on which he had built his formidable reputation with Lancashire. As everything crumbled around him through no fault of his own, he became the scapegoat. He resigned as coach of England and was replaced by Peter Colston, who was formerly the England Under-23 coach.

In their build-up to the Australian international at Twickenham, the selectors devised a curious series of trial matches, which took place on three successive Saturdays in December. In the first match I was picked at lock in the England side that played against the North and Midlands at Leicester. It was not an especially auspicious start for the new coach because the North and Midlands, captained by Peter Wheeler, beat England by 18 points to 10 and the long knives were quickly out and flashing in every direction. The selectors made seven changes in the England side for the next match against the South at Gloucester the following Saturday and I was very relieved to keep my place. We limped home 11–3 in an unspectacular game and the selectors made a further three changes for the grand climax – England against the Rest.

England won this match 39–21 and we were picked en bloc to face Australia a fortnight later. I felt my chances of playing regularly for England depended on where the selectors decided to play Roger Uttley. If they opted to play him at lock as a front jumper, then I was almost certain to be bombed out of the team. But if they preferred Uttley at No. 8, then I had a very good chance of establishing myself in the side. The trouble was that because of the volatile and unpredictable nature of the selectors, I could only survive and plan on a week-to-week basis.

I desperately wanted to win my place entirely on merit but again I owed my selection to an injury to Roger Uttley. He was injured in the match against the North and Midlands and did not make his comeback that season until the morning of the England–Wales match. He then played for Gosforth against Richmond and had the wretched misfortune to break a leg. This cruel twist of fate left the way clear for me to collect another five caps that season, but in only one of those matches did I end up on the winning side.

Australia arrived at Twickenham with a few severe dents in their tour record. They had lost four matches, including the internationals against Scotland and Wales, and we were expected to beat them. Their front row consisted of MacDougall, Horton and Finnane, and England decided the best way to extract retribution for the events seven months previously, and to wipe out all those unhappy memories, was to win the match convincingly. And that is precisely what we did. We recorded our biggest ever win over Australia (23–6) and, under the watchful eye of Welsh referee Merion Joseph, there was no trouble during the match. We scored the only three tries through Barry Corless, Mike Lampkowski and David Duckham, but considering all the ball the backs had, they did not play particularly well. Most of the trouble stemmed from scrum half where Lampkowski was incapable of unleashing a back division. He took time to wind up his pass and even then he lacked length and accuracy. He was a tremendously competitive player, strong on the break, and could bulldoze his way through all but the most determined defence. Unfortunately, at international level, he was confronted by just such a determined defence and, apart from his try against Australia, his contributions were mainly negative.

Much of the blame for this lay with the style of play England adopted. The England pack did extremely well that year and the most sensible tactics, particularly with Lampkowski in the side, would have been to concentrate on ten-man rugby. Cooper and Old, who alternated at fly half, should have kicked for position from set-piece play, while Lampkowski and the back row worked together in close-quarter attacks. Instead, a bold, but completely misguided, policy of spinning the ball wide was pursued with disastrous results.

The great sadness is that Steve Smith, who should have been selected all season, was exactly the type of player England needed to play that style of rugby and to capitalize on the work of the forwards. Smith played well enough in the first two trials, but before these matches he had been told by the selectors to concentrate on feeding the backs and not to try too much on his own under any circumstances. He did just this and was rewarded for his efforts by finding himself demoted to the Rest side for the final trial because, in the words of the selectors, he was not taking people on in the same way as Lampkowski was.

There is no doubt whatever that the best halfbacks in England at the time were Alan Old and Steve Smith, but the selectors somehow managed to avoid playing the two together all season. The nearest they came to playing both men was in the last match of the season against France. Lampkowski was finally dropped and Smith recalled. Martin Cooper was selected at fly half. He had only just recovered from injury and on the Thursday training session he was put through the most punishing fitness test I have ever seen. It lasted well over an hour and even if Cooper had been fit at the start, it is highly unlikely he would have survived intact. Hardly surprisingly, he felt some twinges and the doctors ruled him out of the match. The team naturally assumed that Alan Old, the replacement fly half in the squad of twenty-one, would automatically come into the side to partner Steve Smith. That would have been far too simple and straightforward. Instead, the selectors brought in Chris Williams of Gloucester to win his first and only cap, and any chance we had of finishing the season with a flourish was abruptly ended. It must have been an enormous temptation for Alan Old to pack his bags and disappear there and then, but he said that would have been detrimental to the team spirit and flew with us to Paris to remain on the replacements' bench.

As it transpired our morale was near rock bottom anyway and whatever spirit was left was squashed and eliminated in the Parisian spring sunshine that afternoon. Little did I appreciate back in January that my first international at Twickenham – the match against Australia – was going to be the only victory England were to notch up in my first eight caps. Two weeks later we entertained Wales and not only lost 21–9, but allowed Wales to record their biggest win at Twickenham since 1910. Alistair Hignell kicked three penalties for England, but we spent most of the match on the retreat and were well beaten. J. P. R. Williams scored two tries and Gareth Edwards scored a third after we heeled from a scrum near our line and allowed the maestro to grab the ball and plunge over.

I was still at the stage where I was thrilled simply to be playing and surviving in the side. Though I was disappointed with the result, I did as well as Geoff Wheel at the front of the line-out, thus gaining some confidence for the future. I had begun to adjust to the furious pace of international rugby and contributed as much as any of the tight forwards in the open play. But, in the final analysis, we were up against a side bulging with brilliant backs and we had no one in the same league. It is put in perspective if you analyse the merits of the respective halfbacks – Phil Bennett and Gareth Edwards against Martin Cooper and Mike Lampkowski.

The Welsh used the ball so much better than we did and we failed to change our tactics or alter our course. The gulf that existed in the talent available to both countries was epitomized by the fact that Phil Bennett only came into the Welsh side as third choice. It was in this match that I was made aware for the first time how much tighter the Welsh defence was than ours, and how much better they were able to cope under pressure. They were used to playing under intense pressure at club level week in and week out and they revelled in it. That gulf still exists.

Our chances of winning big matches were severely limited so long as we continued to present the opposition with soft tries, but because of the stirring performances of our pack we set off for Murrayfield in remarkably good heart.

The highlight of that particular afternoon took place shortly before the kick-off when both teams were presented to Her Majesty the Queen and to Prince Philip. That was a great thrill for me and it seemed to inspire our team to perform great deeds in the opening minutes. From the kick-off Ken Plummer on the right wing scampered outside Andy Irvine and looked sure to score in the corner, but he put a foot in touch en route to the line. We continued to attack and in the sixth minute Andy Maxwell scored a try which Alan Old converted. Although Irvine kicked a penalty and converted a try by Alan Lawson, Old banged over two more penalties to give us a lead of 12–9 at half time.

With our pack on top, we should have been able to

consolidate our position, but Lampkowski persisted in attempting a series of suicidal breaks at the base of the scrums and was continually buried and robbed by the Scottish loose forwards. On one occasion I caught the ball from a 22 drop-out, passed it to him and watched him dart five yards in four different directions before being hammered to the ground. When, in fact, he did attempt to add variety to his game by being adventurous and ambitious enough to try passing to his fly half, his basic weakness as a scrum half was fully exposed and he gave a slow, erratic service. To compound our problems, we gave away two soft tries through slack defence under pressure and Scotland ran out convincing winners of a game we knew was there for whichever side was prepared to take its chances.

As our pack had created the better chances, I found it soul-destroying that the backs' play was divided into two categories – cock-ups and mega cock-ups.

It is hard to glean much personal satisfaction from such an encounter, but as I strove to establish myself, it was reassuring for me to perform reasonably well against the guy who was probably the top line-out jumper in Britain at the time – Gordon Brown. It was sad for Scotland that, despite the difficult circumstances, the selectors did not go out of their way to pick Brown even when he was not performing miracles every week for his club. He was a big-match player and on the grand occasion he had no peer at lock forward.

However, we had so many problems with our own selectors, it seems churlish to start worrying about Scotland's difficulties. Our selectors made two changes for the match against Ireland at Twickenham. Mike Slemen won his first cap in place of the injured Duckham and Andy Ripley, who had been winning all the ball at the back of the line-out, was surprisingly dropped in favour of the much shorter Gary Adey. Although we were a little deflated after our traumatic experiences against Wales and Scotland, against Ireland we raced to a 9-point lead with three penalties from Alan Old. He added another in the last minute of the game but, in between, Ireland made the most of their few opportunities to steal a match we really should have won. Tom Grace scored a try and Barry McGann kicked two penalties and a drop goal, but our forwards monopolized possession. Had Steve Smith been at scrum half we surely would have won. Lampkowski was too inexperienced for international rugby and never played for England again. Once again, we were tactically inept in this match. Instead of churning the ball back willy-nilly all afternoon, the forwards should have taken far more on themselves. We should have wheeled, peeled, initiated some back-row moves to suck in and absorb the tearaway, destructive Irish forwards, and relied on Old to keep us grinding forward with accurate line and attacking kicking. The Irish were content to sit on top of our backs and crucify them whenever they tried to run and pass. When Lampkowski broke, he was instantly submerged under a sea of green jerseys.

It seemed impossible to play any worse against France in the last match of the season, but that is exactly what happened in Paris. For the first time that season our pack did not achieve dominance; quite the reverse. We were comprehensively outplayed and humiliated by the best pack I have ever played against anywhere in the world. Steve Smith was, at long last, recalled to the team, but he failed to touch the ball in the opening twenty minutes as France won everything. With Ripley still out of favour, the French threw to Bastiat in the line-out and he mopped up the lot. There was nothing Adey, Wilkinson or I could do to stop him. The selectors must surely have realized this would happen, but they stubbornly and, I think, foolishly left Ripley on the replacements' bench.

The French were so well organized and so explosive, they dominated our throw-in as well as their own and won a lot of ball which they used to drive forward and create havoc in our defence. I have never had such a feeling of hopelessness in a match. They would drive from the line-out into the middle of the field, roll off the maul back to the blind side, and then roll off open again to set up a ruck and set their backs free leaving our forwards battered and demoralized. At the next line-out, as we prepared to defend at the back, they would burst through the middle or peel round the front. I won one line-out early on with a two-handed catch, but by the time I returned to earth, Cholley had turned me round, Paparemborde was holding me in a vice-like grip and Palmie whipped the ball from me before I had the faintest idea what was happening.

They destroyed us in the scrums and I can still picture Mike Burton at tight head being lifted right out of the scrum by the French loose head, Gerard Cholley, and remaining suspended in midair while the French pack drove remorselessly forward. From that sort of tenacious platform, it would have taken an incredibly poor back row not to tie up the second-phase possession. France had the best back row in modern rugby – Jean-Pierre Rives, Jean-Pierre Bastiat and Jean-Claude Skrela.

The staggering fact is that Fouroux had a dreadful game at scrum half, otherwise they could easily have topped 50 points. As it was they ran in six tries and left us in tatters. Afterwards Fran Cotton said it was a case of men against boys and I have certainly never felt so thoroughly inadequate. For the record the French pack that day read: No. 8: J. P. Bastiat; second row: J. P. Rives, J. F. Imbernon, M. Palmie, and J. C. Skrela; front row: R. Paparemborde, A. Paco, G. Cholley. In my estimation, they were the best.

The aftermath of such a crushing defeat was the disappearance of eight members of the England team for ever more. In the pack Gary Adey, Bob Wilkinson and John Pullin never again played for England. Four of the backs were also sunk without trace – Peter Butler, Ken Plummer, David Cooke and Chris Williams.

The casualty list might have been longer, but that was the last game of the season and we had time to regroup and replenish our resources before a new selection committee began its deliberations. I took stock of my record at the end of the season – seven defeats in eight matches. Results have improved since then, but the underlying malaise persists in English rugby and the whole structure desperately needs a drastic overhaul.

The England–Wales match highlighted the two biggest problems which plague the English selectors – the thoroughly moderate standard of club rugby and the sheer size of the country. For that particular game we chose our team from fourteen different clubs, whereas the Welsh side came from just seven clubs. Their pack comprised four from Pontypool, three from Swansea and one from Aberavon. Similarly, Scotland selected their team for the Calcutta Cup match from just seven clubs, which made it much easier for their coach to weld the team together.

The Welsh selectors invariably picked their side almost entirely from London–Welsh and the top ten Welsh Clubs which are all in a concentrated area within fifty or sixty miles of Cardiff. They enjoy a fierce competitive edge by playing keenly contested matches at least once a week at a level consistently higher than even the best English games. Their international players, like the French, are used to playing with players of a high standard against top-class sides every week under extreme pressure. They quickly learn to adapt to that pressure and can comfortably sustain their best form at any level. In the three weeks leading up to the Twickenham international, Swansea had played against London–Welsh, Aberavon and Newport, while I had played for Fylde against Preston Grasshoppers, St Helens, Rugby and Nuneaton. In such circumstances it was not unreasonable to assume that my opposite number, Geoff Wheel, was tuned to a finer pitch and had had a far better preparation. With the exceptions of Leicester and Moseley in the Midlands and Gloucester and Bristol in the south west, we have not had any clubs in the past few years that have consistently been able to live with the best Welsh clubs.

Not only do our clubs usually contain only two or three top-class players along with three or four players adequately versed in the basic skills and at least half a dozen players of extremely modest ability, they play against similarly deficient sides week in week out in matches of a suitably mediocre standard. The better players tend to be dragged down to the desperate level of the average no-hoper. In addition, these clubs are spread over such a vast area, the wretched selectors have to cover hundreds of miles from Devon and Cornwall in the south to the tip of Northumberland in the north trying to guess how good a potential international player is when he's surrounded by poor players and playing against a thoroughly moderate team.

I know of hordes of England players who, between two internationals, can coast through a club match at half cock and still comfortably be the star of the game. That could not happen in Wales or France. This is why we desperately need a greater concentration of our best players in far fewer clubs and then, by regular competition between these elitist clubs, our best players would be far better prepared for international rugby. The country is crying out for a league system and the RFU is stubbornly and doggedly holding back. Evolution comes hard to the Establishment. Everyone accepts that if Liverpool or Manchester United spent half the soccer season playing against teams like Swindon or Chesterfield, their remarkably high standards would inevitably fall. If John McEnroe or Jack Nicklaus spent the majority of the year tackling rookies on the second-class tennis and golf circuits of the world, they would soon find their competitive edge slipping a fraction and then the winning of the handful of really major tournaments would become that much harder.

In all sport nothing is more stimulating than fierce competition and rugby in England should be no different. In Wales and France the top players have to be at their sharpest every week because there is no such thing as an easy or unimportant game. In England, only the

John Player Cup promotes a comparable intensity of interest. Teams prepare far more assiduously during the week of a Cup match than they do at any other time of the season. Leagues would ensure that the better clubs strive towards perfection at least a dozen times a season and that would mean that our international players would be stretched to the limit of their ability at least twenty times a year, including internationals, County Championship games, Cup matches and league games. The alternative is to go bumbling along in the same aimless way in the hope of winning the Triple Crown once or twice every twenty years. For a country of our size and with our playing resources that is criminal underachievement.

In the expectation that the new formula for the County Championship will give the best counties, and therefore, one hopes, the best players, five or six worthwhile games each season, the desperate need for the future is the organization of a league system at club level. I would suggest starting with a national league of two divisions with eleven teams in each, and four regional leagues. The bottom two in the national first division should be replaced by the top two in the second division each season. The bottom two clubs in the second division each year would return to their regional leagues. The top team in each of the four regional leagues would play off at the end of each season, with the winners of, say, the North against the South West and the winners of a play-off between the Midlands and the South securing the two available places in the second division of the national league. The premier league would consist of the eleven best clubs in the country and would attract the lion's share of media coverage and sponsorship money. Such sponsorship would be readily forthcoming and would cover all the travelling and accommodation costs, although with only five away matches each year these should not be prohibitive. These ten league matches each year would bring out the best in all the top players and produce a meaningful championship. The John

Player Cup would provide further intense competition for the best players at club level and the number of Saturdays each year where players could coast through in a carefree and lackadaisical manner would be sharply reduced.

If only one club in the Fylde, Sale, Manchester, Liverpool, Birkenhead Park, Broughton Park, Orrell area managed to win and hold a place in the first division of the national league, then it is reasonable to assume that the best players in that area would eventually gravitate to that club. In this way, sooner or later the top players in the country would be packed into the first division. At the moment not one of the seven clubs listed above would automatically make or survive in the first division. But if all the best players joined the best club, it would produce just as good, if not a much better, side as Leicester, Gloucester or even the top Welsh clubs like Cardiff and Swansea.

Instead of a highly competitive and prestigious national league, the RFU introduced merit tables which have been an appalling waste of time. As a competition they are virtually meaningless. Few people anywhere in the country follow the merit-table results in their own area, let alone show even the slightest spark of interest in any other merit table. Teams can qualify for the following year's John Player Cup through the merit tables, but the rules are so chaotic and the merit tables themselves so disastrously conceived that, according to the RFU *Handbook*, Metropolitan Police qualified for the 1982–83 John Player Cup after finishing tenth and last in the London merit table, having lost every single one of their matches. This farcical situation is by no means unique and illustrates clearly what a worthless competition it is. I know from first-hand experience how clubs prepare for a John Player Cup match and how they treat the normal run-of-the-mill merit-table game and there is a world of difference. The whole charade is further devalued because the merit tables are calculated on a percentage basis as not all the clubs in a table play against each other. The best side never necessarily wins the table and that, indeed, is a ludicrous situation.

From the whitewash of 1976 we steadily improved at international level, but these improvements were made in spite of the system and club structure in England, certainly not because of it. If we are regularly to challenge the supremacy of Wales, France, New Zealand and South Africa, it is incumbent on the RFU to change the system.

8

A Year of Contrasts – 1977

The repercussions of the disastrous international season in 1976 swept through the squad and the selection committee during the autumn. I was looking forward to the new season on the simple basis that, as it was impossible for things to get any worse, we could actually count on some improvement. With the added incentive of a Lions tour at the end of the season, I trained conscientiously during the summer to make sure I could produce top form from the beginning of September.

Lancashire made a bright start in the County Championship, contemptuously brushing aside all opposition to top the northern group with five wins out of five and a convincing points tally of 177 to 36. In January we were to squeeze past Gloucestershire in the semifinal before polishing off Middlesex in the final in grand style. But by Christmas, Lancashire were in invincible form, Fylde were in the middle of their best ever season in the John Player Cup, and I had played for the North and Midlands in their crushing win over Argentina at Leicester by 24 points to 9. Considering Argentina only lost to Wales by 1 point the following week, our win at Leicester was a notable achievement and I felt satisfied that I was playing the best rugby of my life.

I had hoped that my consistent performances at club, county and divisional level would have made some sort of impact on the selectors, but, to my surprise, I was dropped to the Rest side for the final trial at Twickenham. I was bitterly disappointed by this rebuff and for the fortnight leading up to the trial I trained harder than at any time previously. The selectors, in their so-called wisdom, had assembled a fair sprinkling of talent among the 'rejects' in the Rest side, including Andy Ripley, halfbacks Steve Smith and John Horton, Tony Bond in the centre, and Dusty Hare at fullback, all of whom should have been in the England side.

The trial was held on New Year's Day and the players, at least, were models of abstinence and self-denial. On the Friday night we plotted our line-out tactics to confuse the enemy. I was to be stationed at the front, Barry Ayrer in the middle, and Ripley was given a roaming role which worked to perfection. He enjoyed this sort of brief and with the rest of us winning the occasional ball and acting as ideal decoys for Ripley, we dominated the line-out and were level at 3 all at half time. During the interval the selectors made two changes, but they remained blind, oblivious or ignorant to the role Ripley was playing so successfully. Ayrer and I were promoted to the England team in place of Bob Wilkinson and Roger Powell and we ran out comfortable winners in the second half by 20 points to 3.

The new chairman of selectors was Sandy Sanders, a genial man of great discipline and some insight. He was aided and abetted by some new selectors, including Mike Weston, Derek Morgan and Budge Rogers. The revamped selection committee brought to their deliberations a level of commonsense, realism and consistency which had been tragically lacking hitherto, although they were still far from perfect and had a complete blind spot about the consummate skills of Tony Neary.

During my brief involvement with England up to 1977, I had witnessed a whole series of mind-boggling acts of folly that left England beaten before they started. Our team were standing on the first tee 8 over par and there was no way we could claw back that sort of deficit. Although the Moseley halfbacks John Finlan and Jan Webster between them played twenty-four times for England and their careers overlapped, the selectors managed to avoid ever pairing them together in an England side. Such crazy logic earned the results the selectors deserved. Andy Ripley is an example of a player who, if he had been used sensibly by England, and if the selectors had appreciated his great strengths instead of worrying about his limitations, could have won twice as many caps as he did. He could have been as useful to England as Bastiat was to France.

English rugby was littered with such victims right through the seventies. The selectors were guilty of dropping players because they became obsessed with minor deficiencies and ignored unequivocal assets. Peter Dixon and Tony Neary were two other back-row forwards who were shamefully treated. It is interesting to note that at the end of a year in which both Tony Neary and Gordon Brown were spurned and rejected by the national selectors, the great wisdom and perception of the Lions selectors ensured they went to New Zealand. Syd Millar wisely insisted on picking Neary despite the cold-shoulder treatment England's fastest flanker had received from his own selectors and, not unexpectedly, Neary eventually won his place in the Lions Test team. The utter disregard the England selectors showed for Neary's undoubted and unrivalled ability was the one black mark they chalked up early in their reign. Among the most outstanding backs who must have felt high up the selectors' public-enemy hit list during the seventies were Alan Old, Steve Smith and Dusty Hare. The list is long and it would be cruel to mention all the players who were desperately lucky ever to win a cap for England, but the selection of the touring party to Australia in 1975 is symptomatic of the horrific consequences of bad judgement and this was by no means an isolated incident.

Fortunately, under Sandy Sanders, selection improved in 1977 and I feel one of the reasons was that most of the new selectors were more in touch. They had played rugby in the seventies and were in tune with the players' thoughts and the different demands of the modern game.

For the Scotland match the selectors picked a team for a specific job and they were well aware of its strengths and limitations. By choosing the solid Barry Corless and the strapping young Oxford University Blue Charles Kent in the centre, they knew the likelihood of carving holes in the Scottish mid-field with fancy footwork and mystical sleight of hand was slim. But at the same time, the explosive power of Kent could rip asunder the most resolute defence and with these two big men locked together in the middle, our threequarter line had a certain impregnability which had been missing in recent years. If we were not going to score a barrel-load of spectacular tries, we were certainly not going to concede many either. Kent, in particular, had a good season and it was a surprise to me that he disappeared from the international scene the following year. However, he made his presence felt at Twickenham, as did Alistair Hignell at fullback. He was an outstanding defensive player in exactly the same mould as J. P. R. Williams. He had a cricketer's safe hands, a strong tackle and he was absolutely fearless.

After only one win in eight matches, we were not going to give points away easily. To prove it, we only conceded three tries all season and two of those were against Wales at Cardiff. Despite the emphasis on defence, we regained the Calcutta Cup with an exhilarating display in which we recorded our biggest ever winning margin over Scotland and were only one try short of our own post-war Championship record of five tries in one game. Our plan was simple. We reckoned we had much the better pack and decided to exert the utmost pressure in the set pieces. We outscrummaged and outjumped the Scots and then proceeded to dictate the course of events in the loose.

With beautiful ball players like Cotton, Wheeler, Uttley and, above all, Dixon, we controlled the loose exchanges to an almost embarrassing degree and from such a magnificent platform the final outcome was inevitable. We methodically and systematically clamped a stranglehold on Scotland and broke their resistance. With our pack grinding away relentlessly, we put the Scottish backs on starvation diets, and by eliminating our own silly defensive lapses, the team developed some much needed confidence. In the most conclusive England performance for three or four seasons, we scored four good tries. Kent blasted his way through half a dozen would-be tacklers to score one try himself and then he made another for Mike Slemen. Malcolm Young plunged over the line from a beautifully controlled 5-metre scrum and, right at the end, Uttley also powered his way over from a scrum near the line. With Hignell in good kicking form, we won 26–6 and set off for Dublin in excellent heart.

We were in no danger of being overconfident in Dublin. Apart from our miserable overall record in 1975 and 1976, we had not beaten Ireland since 1971. Hopes of an open game were killed by the weather. It was a filthy, overcast day and the match was played in a persistent drizzle on a wet, tacky pitch. For the second time in a fortnight our pack took control and by playing a cautious, dull but efficient game, we denied the Irish tearaway forwards any opportunity to capitalize on our mistakes. We kept plodding down-field with a mixture of driving forward power, tactical kicking from the half-backs Malcolm Young and Martin Cooper, and the odd thundering run from Kent in mid-field. It was not thrilling stuff to watch, but for a new side feeling its way, it was mighty effective. Midway through the second half our reward came when Hignell joined the line in loose play and split the home defence with a neat, angled kick. Nigel Horton hacked on towards the line and Cooper deftly scooped the ball up a couple of metres short and dived over for the only score of the match.

There was much trepidation before the next game against France at Twickenham because the previous year their pack had clinically demolished us in Paris. However, this time we fared very much better against the same eight forwards and, with Nigel Horton

95

outstanding, we should have won. At one stage in the first half we won three rucks in quick succession and I dug my head up from the bowels of the earth to see first Barry Corless and then Mike Slemen squander gilt-edged scoring chances. They cut back inside near the line only to be buried by the cover on each occasion when they had an unmarked player on the outside virtually certain to score. This unfortunate and uncharacteristic error cost Slemen a Lions tour that summer. To compound the felony, Alistair Hignell only succeeded with one of his six penalty attempts at goal and a controversial try by Sangali early in the second half, which included a strong suspicion of a knock-on by Aguirre, was enough to give them a 4–3 win. That evening at the dinner the French players freely admitted that their pack had only played at half prop and England had really deserved to win. It simply goes to emphasize once again that almost every game of international rugby is finely balanced on a knife edge and each match is often hinged on one or two crucial incidents which could go either way. We came infuriatingly close to winning, yet France scraped home and marched on to big wins over Scotland and Ireland to land the Grand Slam for only the second time in their history.

A little deflated, we trudged off to Cardiff to join battle with Wales with a special prize at stake for the winners – the Triple Crown. Not for the first time, and probably not for the last time, our team froze at the Arms Park. That stadium and that Welsh crowd have a magic all their own; many a visiting team now endowed with super self-confidence have become overawed and proceeded quietly to disintegrate. It is interesting that no side in the Five Nations Championship managed to win a single game at Cardiff throughout the period from 1969 to 1981, and yet the All Blacks, during that same time, won on each of the three occasions they visited Cardiff, including a crushing win in 1980. The moral must be that if a team is good enough it will still win, but I remain convinced that playing at home is worth a 6-point start to the Welsh team. We played badly and lost 14–9 and I was annoyed because I did not play well against Geoff Wheel.

This was particularly disturbing as the British Lions team to tour New Zealand was due to be announced a couple of weeks after the Cardiff match and I had been clinging to the belief all year that I might just scrape in as one of the four locks. It was generally acknowledged that Gordon Brown, Nigel Horton and Alan Martin would all be chosen, leaving room for one more front jumper. The Lions selectors chose Wheel and although I was disappointed, I was not really surprised. I only had myself to blame for my poor showing against Wales. As it transpired, Wheel dropped out of the tour shortly before the party was due to leave for New Zealand and I heard on the car radio as I was driving down the motorway that Wheel's replacement had just been announced. At this moment my heartbeat was so strong it was nearly going through the windscreen but when I heard the reporter read out the name of Moss Keane I felt shattered. As Gordon Brown and Keane were primarily, and Martin and Horton were exclusively, middle-of-the-line jumpers, it meant the selectors had decided to set off without a recognized front jumper. That could only mean that they thought there was no one good enough in the British Isles and I took that as a little bit of an affront. At least I now knew exactly where I stood in the selectors' estimation and I promptly went out to book a fortnight's honeymoon in Minorca in July. Hilary and I were married in February 1977 but because of my rugby schedule we postponed our honeymoon. Now that was all settled.

The Lions flew to New Zealand with a fairly strong squad, but it was definitely not the best available. Phil Bennett was a brilliant rugby player by any standards but he was not a suitable choice as Lions captain and he himself has since been critical of his own performance in that very demanding role. Sadly, he was given precious little support from the weak management of George

Burrell and John Dawes. Mike Burton ought to have been selected at tight-head prop and the selectors should have taken Fran Cotton as a loose-head rather than a tight-head prop, along with Ian MacLaughlan rather than Phil Orr. To make three errors of judgement in choosing the four props was not an auspicious start. Among the backs I felt it was criminal not to pick Jim Renwick in the centre and Mike Slemen rather than Gareth Evans as the utility back. I also think Ray Gravell would have been much better suited to the prevailing conditions of an antipodean winter than David Burcher was. To pack more than half the touring team with Welshmen would not have been a mistake if they had all merited their selection, but half a dozen patently had not. On a twenty-five-match tour it is a heavy burden to carry any passengers in a party of thirty-three players and two officials, as the 1977 Lions found to their cost.

More of that anon. When the party flew out of Heathrow, I was left clutching two pieces of paper. One was a letter from the Four Home Unions informing me I was an official reserve on standby during the tour; the other was a paid-up voucher for my holiday in Minorca.

The spring bank holiday weekend found Hilary and myself camping with a gang of friends in the Lake District. We had a good boozy weekend and we talked about the splendid start the Lions had made in winning their first four matches down under. We returned home on the Monday and although my office was closed until the Wednesday, I went in on Tuesday to catch up on some paperwork. The phone rang in the warehouse and I assumed at first that it was a wrong number as it was the Queen's Silver Jubilee that day and nobody could be expected to be working. After a few moments, I crossed the yard and answered the phone to hear Malcolm Phillips, England's representative on the British Lions selection, on the other end.

He told me that Nigel Horton had broken his thumb against Otago and the Lions wanted me to fly out at once as a replacement. My first reaction was one of delight, followed instantly by lingering doubts about my likely role in New Zealand. After all, I was sixth choice and would almost certainly be consigned to a few mid-week games for the dirt-trackers' side, with scant hope of ever making the Saturday side. I was also looking forward to our honeymoon in Minorca, but a reassuring chat with Hilary that night convinced me to pack my toothbrush and head for the other side of the world. Once there, it would be entirely up to me to stake my claim for a place in the Saturday XV.

I put in some hard training during the next three days. I also tried to recover the cost of the cancelled July holiday in Minorca. The travel company pointed out they would be delighted to refund the money if I could produce a medical certificate declaring I was unfit to travel. That little masquerade would have appeared somewhat suspect if the patient simultaneously managed to win a Test place for the Lions on the middle Saturday of the Minorca fortnight! I broached the subject of costs with the secretary of the British Lions and he pointed out that I was meant to be on standby all summer; it was my own fault for trying to fit in a honeymoon before the end of the Lions tour.

On Friday, 10 June, I headed for London to collect my blazer en route for Heathrow. I was accompanied by John Lawrence, the secretary of the Four Home Unions. As we approached Heathrow, traffic ground to a standstill because of a crash on the M4. To catch the flight we had to abandon the car and run the last two miles. John set off in front clutching his umbrella and I pounded along behind with a bag in each hand. None the less, he steadily opened up a commanding gap and, considering he was in his fifties, a huge question mark appeared against my state of health and fitness. I arrived in the nick of time to catch my flight and collapsed in my seat, dripping with sweat and absolutely knackered. I had a journey of a mere thirty-two hours in which to recover.

9

Lions in New Zealand – 1977

I landed at Christchurch two days before the match against New Zealand Universities and was met by Russ Thomas, the New Zealand liaison officer with the Lions. He took me to the team hotel where I had to wait for a couple of hours before the team flew in from Southland. During that time Russ confirmed how well the Lions had been playing to win the first eight games.

I went out to the airport to meet the party and was greeted warmly by the manager, George Burrell, and the coach, John Dawes. All the players came over and welcomed me to the tour except for Willie Duggan. He came up to me, shook me by the hand and told me that if I had any sense at all I would catch the next flight home. He was smiling at the time and the quip was partly tongue in cheek, but there was still a grain of truth in it. The weather had been appalling and some of the hotels in which the Lions had been put fell well short of the normally accepted standard associated with major rugby tours. That combination, and the thought that the tour stretched another two and a half months into the far distance, had left some of the players a little jaded. None the less, no sooner had Willie offered me his tart piece of advice than he received a sharp riposte and rollicking broadside from the management for speaking out of turn.

The next few days proved to be very harrowing for the whole party and for the management in particular. My arrival coincided with the first defeat of the tour, although it would be a trifle unfair to put all the blame on me as I did not actually play in the match. The Lions lost to the Universities by 21–9 and John Dawes tried to extract the utmost retribution at training the following day. That Wednesday's training session in Christchurch, just four days before the first Test, was by far the hardest I have ever undertaken in my life. Considering how little recovery time there was, it was a crazy gamble. The reason the Lions reserve team lost on the Tuesday was certainly not lack of fitness and, even if it had been, that was not a very good excuse for running the Test side into the ground the following day.

I was not 100 per cent fit at the time, although I had kept in strict training during the summer, but if I crashed through the pain barrier about six times in the first hour or so of pure fitness training, I noticed the other thirty guys were faring little better.

Before we left the hotel for the training ground, Dawes warned us the training would be hard but he added that if we decided to do it we would all have to see it through to the bitter end. The players knew he meant business and we ran non-stop for well over an hour. At the end we had to run over to a group of trees about half a mile away and we were given two minutes to recover there before splitting up into backs and forwards for unit skills. During those two minutes, nobody spoke; nobody summoned up the energy to crack a joke or utter a curse – the thirty bodies just lay there mute, knackered and exhausted. Before a burst of unopposed rugby, the forwards scrummaged until every tiny bone and every single muscle ached. When it was all over, we would normally have made a detour of about 150 yards to a small bridge to cross the River Avon to our hotel. On that day, some of the squad just waded across the river in their kit without a word being exchanged.

That night we were still clapped out when we flew up to Wellington for the Test and there is no doubt in any of the players' minds that we lost the first Test on that Wednesday training session at Hagley Park. Come the

Saturday, the team was obviously still leg-weary and, in my view, Dawes must accept the blame for a serious error of judgement.

To make matters even worse, on the next day it was rumoured that, incredibly, he wanted two training sessions just forty-eight hours before the first Test – one in the morning and another in the afternoon. The players rebelled and in the end only one session was held. But to my surprise and disgust that work-out included a series of diagonal runs up and down Athletic Park for half an hour. Many great race horses have lost the Derby because they have left their best form on the home gallops where they have been overtrained. Similarly, great athletes and swimmers at the Olympics have been denied the gold medals that they deserve because they have left their best form on the training track or in the practise pool. Our party were in great form by the following Tuesday but the timing of these fitness sessions was hopelessly, ludicrously wrong; the players were simply unable to raise a gallop on the Saturday.

With Gordon Brown injured, Moss Keane had to partner Alan Martin in the second row although he had not really recovered from the concussion he received in the Christchurch match on the Tuesday. The All Blacks edged the line-out and were faster in the loose, but good goal kicking kept the Lions in contention throughout. The lead changed hands five times and the crucial score came just before half time. The Lions were attacking and had an overlap, but a speculative overhead pass from Trevor Evans was intercepted by Grant Batty, who sprinted half the length of the field to score. Bryan Williams converted to give New Zealand 6 points when the Lions might just as easily have scored.

The All Blacks led 16–12 at the interval and with no further scoring in the second half, they won narrowly on a cold, bleak day. It was not a great game of rugby; we knew we had not played well and yet the scores were still very close. If we could hit our top form in time for the next Test then there was every reason to hope that we could square the series. We had seen nothing at Wellington to daunt or frighten us and we were all convinced that the series was there for the taking. The All Blacks had four big men in the line-out in Andy Haden, Frank Oliver, Ian Kirkpatrick and Laurie Knight, but we had three weeks to sort that particular department out and we were by no means downhearted.

It was at this point that Terry Cobner became the most influential figure in the whole party. Phil Bennett had injured his ribs in the Test and Cobner took over briefly as captain for the next match. He began to drill and organize the forwards and, at once, the pack made rapid improvement. Dawes wisely allowed Cobner to take control of the forwards at training but the disappointing result from this manoeuvre was the lack of progress made by the backs. Dawes was a top-class threequarter himself, but he did not seem able to bring out the best in our backs.

In fairness, it should be stressed that conditions were often so bad because of the persistent rain which plagued the whole tour that it was virtually impossible to play good rugby. Nevertheless, it could be argued that the difference between the two teams was the quality of the respective coaching. For the All Blacks, Jack Gleeson did not miss a trick and brilliantly pulled off the series. There lurked a feeling that if the two coaches had been swapped round, then the Lions would have won by a similar margin of three matches to one.

I have always got on well with John Dawes and I would like to emphasize that I have nothing at all against him personally – quite the reverse – but I think he would admit that he was not always seen at his very best during this tour and, unfortunately, he seemed to let the pressures affect him. He had built up an enviable record with Wales as a player and as a coach, but he failed to grasp the initiative in New Zealand and events quickly overtook him, leaving him a sad figure who, as tour coach, seemed to have lost his sense of purpose and direction.

I think he used his energies in the wrong direction

and was not strong enough to be assistant manager. He did not have a great or particularly beneficial influence and I think he became too preoccupied with himself towards the end of the trip and not involved enough with his players.

I also have great respect for the manager, George Burrell, but he found it hard when the going became a bit rough. Perhaps he was too nice a man. He did not really know the law of the jungle and found himself just a shade out of his depth. If he had been slightly tougher he could have coped much better. However, I found both the manager and coach honest with me in all our dealings and it was disappointing that they both returned home broken men at the end of the trip when it might so easily have been so different. With just a little bit of luck the Lions could well have emulated the excellent record of the 1971 team which was well managed by Doug Smith and Carwyn James.

I played my first game at Timaru against a South–Mid-Canterbury–North Otago select. I was especially keen to play because I had spotted plenty of forward deficiencies in the two matches I had already seen. I was surprised that nearly halfway through the tour, many of the basic set-pieces had not been properly coached. There was no organization at kick-offs and drop-outs, for us or against us, and nobody seemed too sure who was supposed to be doing what. No one was calling for the ball and, not surprisingly, support was lacking if someone did manage to take a clean catch. In the loose some of the players favoured rucking and some favoured mauling and the home sides were taking advantage of our strict adherence to the laws that govern the line-out.

On the eve of the Timaru match, Cobner held a team meeting for the players and no one else. He laid down a well-thought-out plan of campaign to revitalize our play. Our difficulty at the line-out had arisen because we stood in line one behind the other and jumped straight up and down as the law demands, while the jumpers in New Zealand tended to stand half a yard wide of the line-out and leap across the line when the ball was thrown in. We decided to employ these same tactics and they helped to guarantee us a fair share of the ball during the rest of the tour.

I was lucky for that first match. I had Peter Wheeler at hooker to throw in the ball and he knew exactly how I liked it; also Fran Cotton was behind me to make sure I was able to reach my maximum jumping height. So many critics have felt that I jump that bit higher with Fran behind me that I suppose there must be some truth in it. I shared a room with Fran that week and he told me the night before the match that I would always remember Timaru for the rest of my life because that would be the place where I played my very first game for the British Lions. He said he always vividly remembered a little town in Western Transvaal called Potchefstroom where he played in the opening game of the 1974 tour of South Africa.

He was right. I felt 10 feet tall when I sprinted onto the pitch, which was just as well as my opposite number that day, a guy called Ross, was 6 foot 8 inches and dwarfed me at the first line-out. They had a huge pack, but they were technically pretty weak and we rattled up 45 points to win handsomely.

My next match the following Wednesday was another pleasantly one-sided game against West-Coast Buller which we won 45–nil. If this was the shape of things to come, it could be a very pleasant summer.

The only reservations I had concerned the domestic habits of my room mates. We stayed in Westport, a little mining town on the west coast of South Island, and I was left with the short straw when we arrived at the hotel. I was condemned to four nights with Willie Duggan and Moss Keane. What an eye-opener. These two likeable Irish guys are not the most conventional of men. The room was a complete tip from start to finish with all the kit, clothes and laundry hopelessly mixed up all over the place. It was a miracle to find anything amongst the dozens of empty fag packets – a day's supply – numerous empty glasses reeking of stale beer, and empty paper bags which had once held fish and chips or the like. It was a place I can't forget – no matter how hard I try.

The next Tuesday, four days before the second Test, I was amazed to find Gordon Brown playing alongside me at lock in the mid-week no-hopers team against Marlborough–Nelson Bays at Blenheim. A couple of the senior pros took me aside after the team was announced and told me that if I had a good match, I would be in the Test team. I couldn't believe it. Four weeks earlier I had been camping in the Lake District 10,000 miles away, the forgotten sixth-choice lock languishing in oblivion and, suddenly, here I was on the verge of winning a Test place – my ultimate dream in rugby.

It was a warm day at Blenheim and the game was played at a furious pace. We won 40–23, but with both sides running everything, I was absolutely whacked midway through the second half.

I had had a good game up to that point and loved playing with Gordon Brown, but I turned to him at a scrum and said that I was knackered and I couldn't keep the pace up. He looked at me with those big innocent blue eyes and replied, 'We are going into that Test team together, come what may, and every time you slow down or opt out of anything in the next twenty minutes, I'm going to belt you as hard as I can.' He drove me on to the end of the game and it all worked out like a fairy tale. The Test team was read out the next morning and the pack, which included me, showed five changes from the team the management had chosen for the first Test, which shows how far wrong they had been then. Into the side came Derek Quinnell, Brown, myself, Wheeler and Cotton.

The attitude in the Lions camp had hardened noticeably. Some of the most experienced tourists kept off the beer after our win in Blenheim to start the build-up for the Saturday in Christchurch. Our preparation was much better than for the Wellington Test and most of the credit belongs to Cobner. Despite the platitudinous proclamations of all tour managements that until the last week of the tour they have no idea who will be the Wednesday players and who will be the Saturday players, it is essential to find the best fifteen players as early as possible and play them together in all the Saturday games, which, by tradition, are the harder fixtures. In 1977 the management failed lamentably to do this until late on in the tour. It would have been much easier for Cobner to organize the sixteen forwards if they had been split into a Saturday pack and the mid-week pack in the first three weeks of the tour. In fact, this was not done until the sixteenth match. It was hardly surprising the organization was so bad when I arrived, because after eight matches with all the chopping and changing of the teams, no pattern or style was able to emerge.

At last Cobner ended the argument about our loose play. It was agreed to adopt the highly successful mauling techniques that had made the great Pontypool pack feared throughout British rugby. This caught the All Blacks on the hop and enabled us to win the second Test and all our other provincial matches. Unfortunately, we took it one or two stages further and became obsessed with mauling almost as an end in itself. We became involved in rolling mauls and close-quarter work, which ripped the heart out of the provincial sides, but which was dealt with adequately by the All Blacks in the last two Tests. Grinding forward power is all very well, but at the highest level it won't necessarily win matches in its own right; our preoccupation with driving forward power did little to restore the lost confidence among the backs.

It is one thing peeling from a line-out to set up a maul amongst the opposing mid-field trio, roll off back towards the touch line to engage any loose stragglers among the other team's forwards in a second maul, before peeling off back infield to set up another maul, but at some stage the backs have to be given a chance. After the shock in the second Test, the All Blacks were prepared and able to contain these tactics and it meant our backs never received quick possession. Similarly, we scrummaged New Zealand out of the game, but persisted in slow, channelled heels through the legs of the No. 8 to protect the scrum half, thereby greatly reducing the scope offered to our backs. Rolling, driving mauls work well at club level but not quite so well at international level. They so often deprive the backs of quick ball. These tactics have, in my opinion, been the downfall of Lions rugby on the last two tours in 1977 and 1980. The same relentless pressure was imposed at the set scrum where we would drive our opponents back a few metres, pause for a moment before inflicting a second drive on them and then a third. It looked impressive, but it was a slow, methodical process; although it worked a treat in the lesser games where the standard of New Zealand forward play was desperately weak, it proved all too easy for the All Blacks and Springbok Test teams to defend against it. It was a classic example of overkill.

These tactics guaranteed us handsome wins in all the provincial matches, but were partly to blame for our losing the last two Tests. We badly needed some variety and flexibility in our approach and the disturbing thing is that the lessons had not been assimilated by the time we embarked on our South African safari in 1980.

I believe these tactics have gone some way towards eliminating the brilliant individual backs from the British game. From having the best backs in the world in the early seventies, we struggled in New Zealand in 1977.

Another major contributory factor to our overall failure was the lack of a really outstanding scrum half in the Gareth Edwards mould. We needed a player with a fast, accurate service and, infuriatingly, New Zealand had plenty. We had two admirably competitive, gutsy players, but they were not such complete footballers as many of the scrum halves we came across on our travels.

In retrospect, it was a great shame we didn't involve Mike Gibson more during the tour. As a player he was probably past his peak, but our backs could have drawn on his vast experience. As it was, when, incredibly, he was told early on he would be purely a mid-week player, come what may, he lost some of his enthusiasm and gradually drifted out of the limelight and went his own way. I shared a room with him in Wellington and for four days we hardly ever saw each other. Every time I went to our room at night, he was in bed sound asleep and every morning when I woke up, he'd already gone. I never had a chance to speak to him.

The team for the second Test included only one real shock: Peter Squires, who had been playing well with limited opportunities, was dropped in favour of Gareth Evans, who was a much inferior player.

Training went well on the Wednesday and Thursday and there was an air of confidence in the Lions' den that we would square the series. I phoned Hilary, my parents and the office with the news of my selection and then concentrated all my efforts on the match. We worked on our scrummaging and line-out play in mid-week and the preparations went well. The weather had been dreadful in Christchurch all week and the pitch was very heavy. Cobner took the forwards into the shower room a few minutes before the kick-off to psyche us up and remind us of the important task ahead. Unquestionably, he brought out the best in us and with the adrenaline flowing freely we took the field. We made an explosive start and by jumping across and barging at the line-out in exactly the same way as the All Blacks, we began to win most of the ball. In such compressed, claustrophobic conditions, I found it hard to make any two-handed catches, but I was able to palm fairly accurately to Derek Quinnell, who would act as sweeper and did a superb job at tidying up the rubbish at the front and in the middle of the line where Gordon Brown had a great game. He was not as tall as Haden but his timing was immaculate and he was a very athletic jumper for such a big man. Willie Duggan won his share of ball at the back and, with a glut of good first-phase position, we were able to knock the stuffing out of the All Blacks; our pressurized driving in every sphere of the game and a series of punishing rolling mauls stretched and broke their defence. This worked well at Christchurch in the second Test but their wily coach was able to counter our new style by the next Test.

It was a hard, physical, niggly game with the occasional flurry of punches being thrown, but nothing distracted us from our single-minded determination to square the series. Phil Bennett was much more like the commanding fly half we respected and feared in England and he not only slotted an early penalty, but launched an excellent attack from deep inside our own half which led to a try by J. J. Williams. Bryan Williams kicked two penalties for the All Blacks and Bennett replied with two for us which gave us a 13–6 lead at the interval. Near the end Bryan Williams kicked his third penalty to cut our lead to 4 points.

The crowd sprang into life and began to chant 'Black, Black, Black' until the end of the game, but despite some desperate defence we clung on grimly to win. It was a memorable moment to savour and a historic victory – the first time the Lions had ever won the second Test in New Zealand and the first time we had ever won a Test at Christchurch. There were tremendous scenes in the changing room with everyone shaking everyone else by the hand. It was particularly gratifying for the three of us from England who had only just got into the Test side. Terry Cobner, the architect of the triumph, sat in a corner wrapped in a towel and puffing contentedly away on a cigarette with his craggy face wreathed in smiles.

Little did we realize that this was to be the one highlight of the tour on the field of play and our last major victory. The one disappointment that night was the decision not to attend a dance which had been laid on especially in our honour at the Linwood Rugby Club.

Our players just decided they would prefer to stay and celebrate in our hotel. We had previously accepted the invitation and had an obligation to turn up. This was to me a prime example of weak management – something I was determined not to repeat while I was captain of England or of the Lions on a tour overseas. I made sure that the manager and coach on my later tours would know and accept their responsibilities. People in Christchurch had gone to a lot of trouble to lay on entertainment that night and a strong management would have insisted on us turning up.

Four more provincial victories followed before we arrived in Dunedin for the third Test, but our morale had dropped a little because of the endless rain which we had been experiencing. We were often trapped for days on end in our hotel with very little to occupy us; inevitably boredom set in. It was also strange, considering the huge profit the New Zealand Rugby Union were making from the tour, how often we stayed in very moderate hotels. The cumulative effect of the weather and the hotels took its toll and our resistance to adversity was lowered. Long before the end of the tour even the most inveterate of tourists was feeling homesick.

Our Test scrum half, Brynmor Williams, was nursing a pulled hamstring and fighting a desperate battle to be fit in time. He was vital to our cause. In the event, he had to be replaced early in the second half, just when we were getting on top. We fully expected to win beforehand and were very confident, but the All Blacks had made six changes from the team which we had beaten in the second Test and they were a much more formidable outfit. Furthermore, while we intended to employ the same tactics that had been so successful during the previous three weeks, New Zealand changed their approach and won the battle of the coaches handsomely.

For this third Test the All Blacks dropped Sid Going at scrum half and brought in Lyn Davis. He was a very quick, slick passer and a much better link than Going, and this enabled them to move the ball away from our pack. Bruce Robertson had recovered from the injury which caused him to miss the previous international and his generalship and steadying influence were a great comfort to his team. They introduced a new fullback, Bevan Wilson, and a forthright wing in Brian Ford in the backs, a new loose-head prop, John McEldowney, and a new flanker by the name of Graham Mourie. This was Mourie's first international and he was to feature prominently against British teams for the next few years. He had tremendous speed, perception and anticipation and came from the same mould that had created those other brilliant tearaway flankers, Tony Neary, Jean-Pierre Rives and Fergus Slattery. The extra speed Mourie gave them in the loose was really one of the most important differences between the sides, a difference which grew in significance during the next three years as Mourie led the All Blacks on three triumphant tours of Britain in which they never lost a Test. We thought the New Zealand selectors were panicking when they made six changes, but in fact, they were simply strengthening their team.

We got off to the worst conceivable start and I was directly involved. At the first line-out of the game, after only thirty seconds, I jumped in front of Frank Oliver and deflected the ball towards Peter Wheeler. It was not an accurate deflection and the All Black wing, Ford, intercepted and set up a ruck. The New Zealanders won the ruck and to our astonishment they ran the ball. Robertson chipped neatly through and Kirkpatrick scored. Wilson converted. Before half time Willie Duggan scored a try for us and Andy Haden scored one for New Zealand, which gave them a lead of 10–4. But this was not really a fair reflection of the forward domination we had enjoyed in the first half. Part of the trouble was that Phil Bennett had lost his confidence, as had most of the other backs. They tended to run across the field when in possession or allowed Mourie to force them across.

We stuck rigidly to our stereotyped game while they altered their tactics and played in a more adventurous running game. We realized the importance of goal kicking in this match when Andy Irvine and Phil Bennett missed several kicks between them and Bevan Wilson added two penalties in the second half to the conversion he landed in the first. He also dealt remarkably well with the aerial bombardment which we unleashed on him all afternoon in the expectation of unsettling and unnerving him in his first international. A drop goal by Bruce Robertson and a penalty by Andy Irvine completed the scoring. New Zealand won 19–7, to take a 2–1 lead in the four-match series.

Three more easy provincial victories brought us to the final Test in Auckland in mid August. Cobner and Quinnell were injured in the game against North Auckland and their places went to Tony Neary and Jeff Squire. Along with Willie Duggan, this gave us a much more mobile back row and we were able to dominate the forward exchanges even more than we did in the third Test. We came as near as any side could to destroying the All Black pack completely, but they are a mighty resilient rugby nation. They absorbed all our punishment and still had the energy, the wherewithal and the enthusiasm to hit back in injury time to score and steal a notable win.

The All Blacks took the lead with a penalty from Bevan Wilson in the eighteenth minute but the rest of the match until injury time belonged almost exclusively to the Lions. With Morgan and Bennett giving a perfect display of tactical kicking, we spent most of the game on the attack and led 9–3 at half time. Morgan, who played instead of the injured Brynmor Williams, kicked a penalty ten minutes before the interval and then scored a well-conceived try. Neary won the ball at the back of a line-out. Fran Cotton and I combined on the peel to set up a maul in mid-field, tying in the whole of the opposition mid-field trio. We had executed this manoeuvre a hundred times over the years for Lancashire, England and now for the Lions. It left Morgan with the simple task of picking up the ball and scampering over the line to score his third try of the tour. He added the conversion and no one could deny we deserved our lead.

In the second half, they amazed us by using only three forwards in a couple of scrums. This certainly threw us momentarily. They were, apparently, fed up at being pushed around in the scrums and they came up with this ingenious plot to thwart us. We could not, of course, push in the scrum until the ball was put in and no sooner was it put in, than it was out and away. Wilson added a second penalty and, near the end, when some of our kicking began to lose its accuracy, we faltered for the first time in the match. It was to prove extremely costly. Morgan could have won the match for us but, tragically, he missed two reasonably straightforward kicks at goal. Then, in the dying moments of the three-and-a-half-month-old tour, in injury time of the final Test – a match we had at no stage looked like losing – disaster struck.

Steve Fenwick made a mess of taking our mark when all we needed in order to win the match was for him to find touch. The referee correctly gave them a scrum, which New Zealand won, and Doug Bruce kicked to Gareth Evans. He dropped the ball. Bennett, covering diligently, collected the ball but then failed to find touch with his kick. The All Blacks hoisted an up-and-under which Fenwick caught but then passed to Wheeler who was in a worse position. Wheeler looked stunned by Fenwick's indiscretion and when he was bowled over by Mourie, the ball broke to Knight who scored in the corner. It was 10–9 to New Zealand. Fourteen weeks of hard graft went up in a puff of smoke. Two lapses of concentration undid all the magnificent work of the pack. It was hard to believe we had crushed the All Blacks up front in two successive Tests, only to lose both. As I was choking back the disappointment, I looked round and saw Phil Bennett in tears. Our great dream had been shattered, and although I, personally, had had a satis-factory tour on the playing side, I was every bit as bewildered and brokenhearted as the rest of the party at the result of the final match and the outcome of the series.

For the players there would always be another chance, another day. But George Burrell and John Dawes are likely to go down in history as the two nice guys who led the 1977 Lions, and let them down badly with weak, ineffective management. Their plight and fate was summed up when Clive Williams, the loose-head prop, tore his knee ligaments and had to be replaced. It was imperative to send for a tight-head prop because Fran Cotton had switched during the tour to play at loose-head. When Charlie Faulkner was summoned, Dawes had managed to land himself with three loose-head props and only one tight-head for the last chunk of the tour. They should have sent for either Mike Burton or Sandy Carmichael.

In the final analysis I suppose I felt sorry for Dawes because I thought he failed to cope with the biggest challenge of his life. I thought he became too sensitive and tended to overreact to any criticism, whether it was justified, as it often was, or not. He had coached a great Welsh side but that team was so choc-a-bloc with talent that it was not that difficult; in fact they didn't need a coach at all to win the Championship. The 1977 Lions saw him under pressure for the first time as a coach and he failed to deal with it comprehensively. He became petty on many occasions and allowed himself to become involved in a personal vendetta against the press for no good reason. Along with many of the players, I was especially disappointed in his attitude to the tour and in his lack of ability as a coach. Like many of the other players on the tour, including the backs, I can honestly say that I learned absolutely nothing from him in two months on tour. We needed a big man at the helm and Dawes did not fulfil that role. If Carwyn James had coached the 1977 Lions we would surely have won the series.

10

Captain of England – 1978

I returned home from New Zealand a much more
assured and confident player because I had managed to
win my place in the Test team. Despite a pretty torrid
ten weeks of tough rugby, I was looking forward to the
start of the new season. I had greatly benefited from
playing with so many good players and appreciated the
experience of playing in the highest class of rugby.

I had intended to have a complete break from rugby
until early October but for two very good reasons I
hardly had any break at all. In the middle of September
I was chosen to play for the British Lions against the
Barbarians at Twickenham in a special match to celebrate the Queen's Silver Jubilee and a month later I
was invited to captain an England XV in an international against America.

The Jubilee match raised £100,000 for charity and it
was, as expected, a spectacular affair. However, the
events leading up to it were not without incident because
there was a fair amount of controversy amongst the
Lions about the attitude of the organizing committee
towards the players' wives. We resented the fact that
such a jamboree match was going to be treated in exactly
the same way as an international game and our wives
were not going to be invited to join in the celebrations
until late on the Saturday night after the dinner. The
players firmly believed that their wives should be
allowed to come on the Thursday and share in the whole
weekend. In the end the rugby authorities pieced to-

gether a shabby compromise which allowed our wives to join us on the Friday, as long as we stayed at a less fashionable hotel than usual. Honour was more or less satisfied and nothing, not even that niggly little confrontation, could detract from a unique and memorable occasion.

Both teams were introduced to Prince Charles before the match and he asked me about my head band. He wondered if it was to keep my ears warm or just to stop people pulling them or whatever. It certainly paid to wear the head band: I was one of the few players he engaged in conversation. Exactly the same thing happened two years later when I was introduced to Prince Philip before the Calcutta Cup match. I had half a mind to wear it when I went to the Royal Garden Party at Buckingham Palace in the expectation that the Queen would feel obliged to make a polite inquiry, but perhaps that would have been carrying my trade mark a little too far.

The match produced a high-scoring, swashbuckling game of rugby which we won by 23 points to 14. No sooner had I finished that exhibition game and begun my intended short break from playing than Malcolm Philips phoned me up to ask if I would like to play against the touring American Eagles at Twickenham in the middle of October. He mentioned that the selectors had sensibly decided to choose an experimental XV very much with an eye to the future, but they felt it was essential to include a handful of experienced campaigners in case things went wrong during the match. I said I was quite happy to play if they really wanted me to and he told me he would confirm everything the following Monday morning. I mentioned that I was down in the south on business all day on the Monday and it would be best for me to give him a check call in the afternoon.

When I phoned Malcolm I received the biggest shock of my rugby career. He told me that I had been chosen as captain. Not since my school days had I ever been asked to captain anyone. It came as a complete shock, but I assumed it was just a one-off situation which had no special significance. I never gave it any further thought that afternoon as I drove to a business meeting in Harlow.

It was there that I realized the responsibilities the job carried. Half a dozen rugby reporters were on the telephone waiting to interview me. Once it had sunk in that I was to captain England at rugby, even a slightly diluted international team, I felt very excited and honoured. I was determined to make a decent showing. Some of the usual pressure was removed because it was not a full international. We only met and trained on the Friday afternoon rather than on the Thursday which left me only twenty-four hours to worry and brood about my new role as a leader of men. In fact, we prepared in a very relaxed atmosphere and I adopted a low-key role as captain. Peter Dixon was also in the side and we were both so much older and more experienced than the rest I did not feel too nervous when it came to the team talks in the hotel and in the dressing room. I think I was less emotional than Henry V before Agincourt, but we went out and played as well as any experimental scrap side could have been expected to perform, winning comfortably by 37 points to 11.

I quite enjoyed my new role and was delighted to receive what, I suppose, amounted to a vote of confidence, when I was invited to captain the North of England in the Inter-Divisional Championship. That again was not a thorough and exhaustive examination of my qualities as a captain because we won both our matches convincingly. We scored 50 points against the London Division in a hopelessly one-sided contest, which emphasized conclusively where the great strength of English rugby lay. Then, in the final, we beat the Midlands 22–7.

I was pleased with these three results under my captaincy but it seemed highly unlikely that such a novice in this new and demanding world would be given the leadership of the full England team. I thought at the time that either Fran Cotton or Peter Wheeler should really have been made skipper, but I learned how serious the selectors were when they appointed me captain of the England team against the Rest in the final trial. That was not a very distinguished game, ending in an unspectacular 15–15 draw with only one try scored and that by the Rest, not us.

However, although I had never really had any ambition to captain England, or any other major team, I was not daunted by the prospect. So I was pleased and thrilled when it was announced that I would lead England against France in Paris in the first international of the 1978 season. In those days, it was mostly a nominal role which involved a brief team talk immediately before the match and the responsibility of making the occasional decision during the game. As my reign as captain continued, I became increasingly involved until, by the end of my span, the selectors and coach would actually consult me before picking the team or deciding on the tactics to be employed in any given match.

For that first match in Paris we had a squad session the previous Sunday which included a practice game against Buckinghamshire. Our scrummaging was a trifle suspect and there was a little bit of needle in the hooking duel because Peter Wheeler was confronted by the England team physiotherapist, Don Gatherer, in the Bucks team. Gatherer actually took two strikes against the head, which scarcely helped us to build up confidence to face France. Even more serious, Cotton injured his knee and was forced to drop out of the international against France; he also missed the match against Wales.

Our preparations received a further setback when the combination of a strike and heavy snow on the Thursday left fourteen of the team stranded in London and Nigel Horton in Paris. This meant Horton missed our main practice session but at least we were able to do some scrummaging at Richmond with Cotton's replacement – Mike Burton. He was an experienced and respected international and during the session he said that there was no way our pack would be good enough to take on the magnificent French forwards; we should concentrate on spinning the ball out to the backs as fast as possible to see what sort of progress they could make.

At that moment I decided to have my say as captain. In full view of the entire squad I looked him straight in the eyes and insisted that if we were to have the remotest chance of success it was imperative to take the French on up front throughout the match. If we decided to play second fiddle we would be crucified and humiliated. I made it clear that I was perfectly prepared to scrummage myself into the ground to help Peter Wheeler and to contest every single line-out, causing as much inconvenience as possible to Palmie if I was not actually able to win the ball myself.

I realized that, almost unwittingly, I had asserted my authority as captain for the first time and had issued some sort of rallying call to the troops. It did not pass unheeded. Mike Burton quickly supported me and it was agreed we must take on the French in a man-to-man head-on confrontation from the kick-off. Our resolve was unanimous.

We spent a quiet day in Paris on the Friday and in the evening we had our usual eve-of-match team meeting. Over the years I had heard a lot of passionate team talks from various captains on the Friday night, but I felt much of the impact was wasted eighteen hours before the kick-off, so instead I allowed our coach, Peter Colston, and the chairman of selectors, Sandy Sanders, to do most of the talking.

I saved my little oration and call to arms until a quarter of an hour before the kick-off in the changing room. I had a few points I wanted to make and tried to build everyone up to play their hearts out for their country. In a sense, some of the pressure was missing because we were very much the underdogs. Our mission would be considered partly successful if we managed to give the current Grand Slam Champions a run for their money at home.

We had not won in Paris for fourteen years and in our previous four cross-Channel visits we had conceded 114 points which included three crushing defeats. Although we lost 15–6 that day, we played pretty well although we were handicapped by three severe injuries just before half time. Andy Maxwell damaged a knee so badly that he never played rugby again and Peter Dixon hurt his collar bone. They were both replaced, but when, early in the second half, Robin Cowling dislocated a shoulder, he had to stay on because we had used up both our replacements. It was a brave decision on Robin's part. He must have been in great pain but his action typified the tremendous spirit in the side. Considering these circumstances, we could be well satisfied with our performance as we actually led France 6–3 at half time before the spate of injuries disrupted our rhythm.

At the dinner I was nervous about making a speech, not sure whether to try to fumble my way through in pidgin French or play safe and stick to simple English. Former England and British Lions scrum half Dickie Jeeps told me not to worry either way as the translator would make a complete hash of it anyway. He was right – he did.

We left the dinner late in the evening and spent a great night with the French players at the Moulin Rouge. That was the last opportunity I had to relax during the next fortnight as we prepared for another major uphill struggle – Wales at Twickenham. Alan Old, who scored all our points in Paris with two drop goals, and had had a fine game at fly half, was, surprisingly, dropped in favour of John Horton, Bob Mordell replaced the injured Peter Dixon, and Barry Nelmes took over from the courageous Robin Cowling, who was out for the rest of the season.

The weather brought back memories of New Zealand. The game was played on a saturated pitch which ruled out any possibility of decent rugby and the outcome was decided on the ability to kick penalties in dreadful conditions both overhead and underfoot. Phil Bennett kicked three goals out of four attempts while poor Alistair Hignell was only successful with two kicks out of six, including a relatively straightforward one which would have levelled the match at 9 all. To lose 9–6 was disappointing but we were not too despondent to have lost our two most difficult matches narrowly.

The first really embarrassing moment for me as captain came at the dinner in the evening. I had jotted down three major points to make. Phil Bennett had deservedly been made an MBE in the Honours List; the match had been Gareth Edwards's fiftieth game in succession for Wales; and the weather was as bad as in New Zealand. I was the last person to speak and the first three people comprehensively covered all my points. I rose to my feet and very nearly dried up. But, panic-stricken as I was, I managed to start with a half decent line. The previous speaker, in congratulating Gareth on his fiftieth cap, talked about his remarkable promise as a schoolboy and how he remembered him starring in a particular match. I began by suggesting there was probably no one in the room who could honestly claim to have been old enough to have watched Charlie Faulkner as a schoolboy. In the programme that day Faulkner claimed to be thirty-five and, give or take twenty years, no one would have disagreed. I very quickly thanked Wales for the game and sat down.

We had a month before the Murrayfield match and that turned out to be, in a sense, the battle of the 'minnows'. Scotland had lost their previous three games and for them this was the last opportunity to avoid the humiliation of a whitewash. For me, it no longer seemed to matter if I played well or not; but I still experienced a horrible, empty feeling if I captained the team to a defeat. I was desperate to finish the Championship with a couple of wins and thankfully we won at Murrayfield for the first time for ten years and scored our first two tries of the season. With Cotton and Dixon fit again after injury, our pack overwhelmed the Scottish forwards and we denied them any sort of decent possession.

We had spent much of the previous Thursday afternoon scrummaging at Peebles against the local pack. At first we pushed them all over the place, but after a quarter of an hour we could hardly move them back at all. Fran Cotton complained that his opposite number seemed to be getting stronger all the time and there was not enough weight coming through from the second row. I was giving it everything I could, but we seemed to be fairly static for twenty or thirty scrums. The reason became clear when we broke up. The Peebles pack had gradually expanded and been supplemented. We were scrummaging against sixteen forwards and still pushing them back a fraction. That was the sort of invincible powerhouse our scrum had become.

The one important decision I had to make in the Calcutta Cup came just before half time. We were leading 6–0 and had a penalty from over 50 metres out and at an angle. That afternoon Malcolm Young converted both our tries by Peter Squires and Barry Nelmes, but his forte was accuracy from short range and our fullback, David Caplan, was not a recognized goal kicker. Neither was Paul Dodge in the centre, but I knew he had a fair boot on him so I chucked him the ball, wished him luck and told him to have a whack. Apparently the chairman of selectors, Sandy Sanders, said to his colleagues that I must have taken leave of my senses, but at that moment the ball sailed between the posts and he immediately remarked that I had, of course, made an eminently sensible decision.

At last I was able to make a winning speech at the dinner, something I was to repeat a fortnight later when we beat Ireland at home by 15 points to 9, again scoring the only two tries of the match through Peter Dixon and Mike Slemen. Our forwards produced another stirring performance and we finished the season in a semi-respectable position in the middle of the championship table. There were a lot of improvements still to be made, but we were moving in the right direction and, to my surprise, I had enjoyed my new job as captain.

It was not, unfortunately, to last indefinitely. I led the North of England to a big win over Argentina at Headingley in October 1978, but in the unofficial international at Twickenham ten days later we only drew with Argentina 13–13. A month later we were to meet New Zealand at Twickenham and I don't think a side has ever gone into a major international in recent years worse prepared.

After Lancashire lost to Northumberland in the County Championship a week before England played New Zealand, the England coach, Peter Colston, came up to me as I was walking to the changing room and asked me what I thought we ought to do at our training session on the Thursday and Friday immediately before the international. I was glad to be asked but annoyed that we only had two days to prepare for such an important game. Incredibly, we were the only country who did not have any squad sessions before we played New Zealand on their major tour of Britain in 1978, and as our team preparations for the match against Argentina had been poor to say the least, we started at a major disadvantage.

We received another severe setback when Fran Cotton tore his achilles tendon in October. None the less, the selectors made matters far worse by picking a recognized loose-head prop, Barry Nelmes, to play at tight-head. It was a crazy decision which was never to be repeated. As if that was not a big enough disaster, John Scott was picked to partner me in the second row. Scott, who was an outstanding No. 8 and nothing else, was never to win another cap at lock. This was to enable the selectors to pick Uttley at No. 8, but he had only recently recovered from injury and should not have been considered for this match. .

Given this lop-sided pack, we were on a hiding to nothing. Naturally we were outscrummaged and outplayed in the loose by a very good New Zealand team.

We assembled at Bisham Abbey on the Thursday and trained there in the afternoon. On the Friday we went by coach the thirty-odd miles to London for afternoon tea and to a theatre show in the evening. By the time the coach returned to Bisham Abbey, it was midnight before the team went to bed – not the ideal preparation to face a New Zealand side which had already beaten Ireland and Wales and was en route to a historic Grand Slam.

On the Saturday morning we had a late breakfast and then had to face another coach journey to Twickenham. We were thumped 16–6 by Mourie's All Blacks and it could have been an awful lot more. They could easily have doubled their score if they had not decided to coast through the second half and they made our pack look thoroughly inadequate. At the dinner in the evening I sensed all was not well. I felt I was getting the cold shoulder treatment from the RFU hierarchy. It soon dawned on me that I was going to be made the scapegoat for all the howlers that the selectors had made and, sure enough, I was relieved of the captaincy. To me it was a little like putting Jackie Stewart in a Mini Metro and, when he failed to win the British Grand Prix, sacking Stewart rather than changing the car.

The following Saturday I salvaged some pride when the North of England put up a spirited fight before losing 9–6 to the All Blacks and I enjoyed playing for the Barbarians in the last match of the tour when we lost by just 2 points in a high-scoring game. I was relieved when the teams for the final trial were announced that I was still in the England side, although the captaincy had passed to Roger Uttley. I was slightly mystified that Roger should take over; he had only just won his place back in the team and he was actually not playing that well. One of the selectors, Malcolm Phillips, broke the news of the trial teams to me on the telephone and I was so annoyed to lose the captaincy that I went straight out and ran ten miles to work off my aggression and frustration. However, that trial was curiously split into three sessions and at the end of the second session, Uttley retired with a bruised thigh. I was reinstated as captain, but not for long. After the trial the team was announced for the first international of the season against Scotland and Roger Uttley was named captain. Our forwards annihilated Scotland, but we only drew 7–7. Our backs showed little penetration and Neil Bennett missed four kickable penalties. Ten minutes from the end of the match Uttley injured his leg again and was replaced by John Scott, with the captaincy passing to me.

For the match against Ireland two weeks later, Uttley was again chosen as captain but he withdrew with flu on the morning of the match. I again took over and held the captaincy for the next four years until my retirement. The various machinations of the previous two months had hardly helped my authority and my self-confidence was at a very low ebb. Worse was to follow ten minutes before the Irish game. After a brief consultation with the senior players, I decided with their approval that if I won the toss we would play against the wind in the first half. Having got the support of the players for this decision, I was about to leave the changing room when the selectors came in en masse and told me to play with the wind if it happened to be my choice. I won the toss and followed their instructions. We lost 15–6. The players were disappointed and I vowed never again to be a lackey for the selectors. In future I would always be my own man, make my own decisions, and stand or fall by them. If I was wrong, the selectors could get rid of me, but at least I would go doing what I believed was right.

I was reappointed captain for the French game and insisted that we had a Sunday squad session before the match. We practised hard and, against all the odds, beat France 7–6. They were the current Champions, had already beaten Wales and were certainly expected to beat us. Nigel Horton, John Scott and I cleaned the French out completely at the line-out and with this one result I had firmly re-established myself as captain. We failed dismally against Wales at Cardiff in the last match of the year, but with Budge Rodgers appointed the new chairman of selectors for the following season and Mike Davis as the new coach, plus the prospect of an England tour to the Far East in May, I was able to look forward to the immediate future with great optimism.

11

From Tokyo to Otley in Triumph – 1979

The preparations for the 1980 season began with our seven-match tour to the Far East in May 1979. Budge Rogers and Mike Davis were in charge of England for the first time and though they picked an experimental party, they could afford to take a few gambles for the future as the opposition was not going to be very strong. We knew that there would be a few easy games and there would be no risk of another disaster similar to the Australian tour of 1975. Budge and Mike impressed me enormously with the thoroughness of their preparations for the trip which turned out to be one of the most enjoyable tours of my career.

We almost came a cropper in the second match of the tour. It took a late try by Peter Squires and a conversion from Dusty Hare to enable us to beat Japan 21–19 at Osaka. That match apart, we won every game comfortably and finished up scoring 270 points whilst conceding only 93. We won the second Test against Japan 38–18, but again it was impossible not to admire the incredible ingenuity of the Japanese forwards who employed a thousand and one different ploys to compensate for their lack of size.

In that second match of the tour, against Japan in Osaka, I found myself at the first line-out opposite a little chap of 5 foot 8 inches. I assumed I was going to be in for a very easy afternoon. At that moment the ball was thrown in to the feet of the Japanese prop who was standing at the front of the line-out. He jumped up in the air to allow the ball to continue its journey and the guy opposite me at No. 2 in the line bent down to collect the ball and form a ruck at one and the same time. What made the whole bizarre situation even more ludicrous was my own rather inadequate reaction. As I saw the hooker about to release the ball on the throw-in, I took the not altogether unreasonable decision to jump for the ball on the assumption that even if he was throwing to the midget at No. 4 in the line, I could probably still get a hand to the ball. This resulted in the farcical situation of my being suspended in midair while Konodo was grovelling on the ground winning the line-out.

I have always had great respect and admiration for the adaptability of the Japanese and their line-out play was a constant source of bewilderment to us. They had so many variations of two-, three- and four-man line-outs, with guys rushing in every direction, that they were able to win a lot of their own ball. It was a model lesson to everyone that you do not have to be 6 foot 6 inches to be a good line-out player.

Another clever ruse was to have three or four players jumping up and down at different times while the hooker prepared to throw in. This meant we had to jump a fraction later to be ready to counteract them. Then, suddenly, the hooker would throw in to one of his players who was back with his feet on the ground ready to jump, whilst the opposing England player was still on his way down after an early false jump. It was all fiendishly clever. They did everything except encourage a straight jump between two players, as they knew there was no way they could win that.

At a time when coaching in England had been in a state of stagnation for a number of years, with the forwards grinding away remorselessly and the backs ploughing through a series of dull, predictable moves, in some far-off corner of the rugby world the game was genuinely displaying touches of originality and making good progress. The Japanese will always be too small to beat giant teams such as the All Blacks or any of the British sides, but they taught us a thing or two about support play with their tremendous fitness and speed round the pitch and their total commitment to defence. They tackled fiercely and scrummaged aggressively, despite giving away 20 stones or more. Their technique and compactness made it extremely difficult for us to ever push them off their own ball and they have remained an intriguing example of what enlightened coaching can do.

We won both our games in Fiji because the Fijians made the fatal mistake of trying to play us at our own game instead of throwing the ball around in the marvellous, carefree, yet extremely skilful, way that has become their trademark. In the final match we beat Tonga in a fast open game on a dreadful pitch. When we trained there the day before the game we noticed that there were a lot of holes and insisted that these be filled in for the match. The Tongans complied with our demands – they simply went down to the beach, carried back buckets of raw coral and shingle and filled up all the holes. Such was the roughness of the end product, that it dissuaded one or two of our less heroic souls from producing any kamikaze tackling.

The tour was useful in several key ways. In a negative sense it proved conclusively that half a dozen players were not up to international standard and they could be discarded from the minds of the selectors in the future. It was certainly a bonus to find out that sort of information on an unbeaten tour of the Far East rather than in a full international against Wales at Cardiff. On the positive side, Huw Davies played exceptionally well in all the big matches and showed himself unquestionably to be a player for the future. John Carleton came through as a high-class wing and began to mount a serious challenge to Peter Squires. Nigel Pomphrey began to look the part at flank forward; however, after the tour he returned to playing at lock for Bristol and that ended his international pretentions. Paul Dodge and Maurice Colclough both confirmed their abundant promise and Ian Peck had a very good tour at scrum half to maintain his challenge for a place in the England squad.

The month on tour also gave our new coach, Mike Davis, an opportunity to exert his influence. For him it was like a four-week squad training camp with a few practice matches thrown in for good measure. For some of our veterans Mike was initially a little bit too much of a school master, but he readily adapted his approach and had soon won everyone's respect. It speaks volumes for him that, after years of coaching schoolboys, he was able to adjust so quickly to knocking a national side into shape. There is no doubt in my mind, or indeed in Mike's, that the ground work for our Grand Slam season was firmly laid on that Far East tour.

Two months later I left England again on another major tour which was to have a significant bearing on England's international season. The North West Counties went to South Africa in August. Because I had to take my summer holiday to go on this trip I took Hilary with me so we could have some sort of break together. It proved an interesting exercise; Hilary realized that a rugby trip is not all glamour and glory, but a lot of hard work combined with the demands of moving towns every three days and living out of a suitcase.

Des Seabrook was the coach. He had at his disposal the core of the England back division – Steve Smith and John Horton at halfback, John Carleton and Mike Slemen on the wings, and Tony Bond in the centre. It was also the trip on which Fran Cotton was able to prove his fitness after twelve months on the sidelines with achilles tendon trouble. It was a physically demanding, gruelling tour, with games against Western Province, Natal, Orange Free State, South East Transvaal and Northern Transvaal. It gave Smithy the chance to get fit, lose some of his excess weight, and thus ensure his return to the England team. Fergus Slattery had said earlier in the year how hard it must be to impersonate a scrum half when you have the build of a prop forward. Since that tour, Smithy has never looked back. Our forwards adopted the same style of play as we had used to destroy opponents on the Far East trip and which we were to use so successfully three months later against the All Blacks in our historic win at Otley. We drove at them in the set, rolled off from the mauls and picked a fast set of loose forwards to help us dominate the open play. Our pack in South Africa was built round Fran Cotton, Peter Dixon and me. It was an excellent preparation for the All Blacks game. We all returned home super fit and, thanks to rugby, I was able to look back on two excellent summer holidays.

I was pleased because I had tremendous faith in Budge and Mike. That faith was rewarded early in November when the selectors invited me down to Leicester one weekend for informal discussions on a squad training session a month before the international against New Zealand. This was an entirely different working relationship to anything I had experienced before. They even had the courage to appoint me captain then, a full month before the international. At long last the selectors made it clear that they had confidence in me and not only did I now have confidence in the selectors, what is even more important I had confidence in myself.

After all the ups and downs of the previous few years, everything seemed to be coming together. I was relishing the prospect of leading England that season. Lancashire were playing some superb rugby to win the Northern Division of the County Championship in a hack canter en route to eventually thrashing Surrey in the semifinal and beating Gloucestershire in the final. The North were making the most thorough preparations for their match against the All Blacks a week before the international, and the confidence of Mike Weston, the chairman of the North selectors, that we had a great chance of winning spread right through the squad.

The Midlands had tried to run the ball against the All Blacks and they had been murdered by 30 points.

At my informal meeting with the England selectors, we agreed it would be foolish to try to play that type of game with our resources. We concluded that we would have to take them on up front and give them no opportunities to counterattack. The Northern Division decided on exactly the same tactics under the skilful coaching of Des Seabrook and the team was picked accordingly. We decided to play ten-man percentage rugby, fully committing the All Blacks pack and taking no risks whatsoever. For the month preceding the match we had a weekly training session at either Headingley or Roundhay; by the end every single player knew exactly what his job was and how the other fourteen depended on him not to let them down. Mike Weston deserves the utmost credit because he had a bit of pressure put on him from the England selectors to pick one or two individuals whom they wanted to see with an eye to the future and he resisted this strongly.

The first prerequisite was for a kicking fly half and we had at our disposal the best in the business – Alan Old. There was no one in the country better suited to keeping his team going forward, nursing his own pack and pinning down the opposition with a masterly display of tactical kicking. Peter Dixon was chosen at No. 8 because he was the best distributor of the ball from the scrum and it was imperative to give Steve Smith and Alan Old as much time and room to control the game as we possibly could. We had the strength of Roger Uttley at blind-side flanker and the speed and enterprise of Tony Neary on the open side. Jim Sydall and I were unlikely to give much away at lock, and we had a very solid and experienced front row – Colin White, Andy Simpson and Fran Cotton.

The overall pace and anticipation of the New Zealand loose forwards – Ken Stewart, Murray Mexted and Graham Mourie – had proved irresistible as they piled up seven successive wins but by keeping the game tight, we felt we could freeze them out. At fly half they had picked a runner in Eddie Dunn and we had a few crash tackling thunderbolts like Tony Bond to bring to an abrupt halt any attempts at fancy handling moves. On the few occasions the All Black centre, Murray Taylor, had a go, Bondy cut him to ribbons with some spectacular tackling. It was inspiring stuff. For once in our lives everything had been worked out to the finest detail and it all came off.

The atmosphere was fantastic at Otley, with a few thousand more people than official capacity, packed like sardines into the ground. They were festooned on trees all round the ground, on every roof and vantage point which offered a view of the pitch, and they were hanging like monkeys on the gantry and scaffolding of the BBC radio and television commentary boxes. I have never before or since experienced an intensity of passion like it and we were desperate not to let our supporters down. It was a filthy, wet day with a strong wind, which the All Blacks had behind them in the first half, blowing down the pitch. But with our pack in scintillating form, we dominated the game throughout. We drove them in the scrums, peeled and rolled from the line-out, drove again in the loose where we outmauled them and when in trouble, Smithy and Old kicked brilliantly for position. We only gave the backs quick loose ball after we had first of all sucked in Mourie, Mexted and Stewart and safely tucked them at the bottom of a maul out of our way.

Mourie and Mexted revelled in fringing around the forward play and then ripping into the opposition's mid-field players. We made sure they were committed to tackling our forwards for eighty minutes until they were utterly exhausted and thoroughly fed up. To their credit, they stuck manfully to this distasteful and alien task, but it left our backs with the freedom of the park when we did decide to spin the ball from the loose on a very few, carefully selected occasions.

When the All Blacks won the ball they began to panic and we soon reduced them to tatters. It was fantastically satisfying to take part in such a clinically successful, brilliantly masterminded operation. The brains behind this operation were Mike Weston and Des Seabrook; on the field there were fifteen heroes. Sydall had the game of his life against Haden and we enjoyed the better of the exchanges in every phase of forward play. Playing with the wind, the All Blacks fullback, Richard Wilson, missed several kicks at goal and we hit back to score. Steve Smith split their defence open with a beautifully angled kick which caught Richard Wilson and Stuart Wilson in a dither. Mike Slemen sprinted through, collected the ball and put Smithy over near the posts. Old banged over a penalty and at half time, having played into the teeth of the wind, we were leading 7–0.

I remember saying to the team at half time that if we all lived and played until we were a hundred years old we would never again have a better opportunity of beating the All Blacks. That, of course, was tempting fate and right at the start of the second half Richard Wilson kicked a penalty. The next twenty minutes, though, were a glorious patch for English rugby. Tony Bond went thundering over for two tries and Old converted one of them to give us a commanding lead of 17–3 midway through the half, leaving the New Zealanders shellshocked and reeling. A quarter of an hour from the end of the game they staged a brief rally. Stuart Wilson scored a try which Richard Wilson converted, but by then they were a well-beaten team.

Appropriately we had the final word when our pack pushed them off their own ball at a scrum near their line. Smithy scissored with Old and the fly half capped an outstanding match with a splendid try. The crowd had given us tremendous encouragement and inspiration and we had repaid them with one of the greatest ever performances by an English side. The famous former All Blacks coach, Fred Allen, said afterwards that it was the best display he had ever seen anywhere in the world by a side against the All Blacks.

We carried out our prearranged tactics down to the last detail and it was one of the most satisfying games of my career. It was Peter Dixon's last big match and he could not have ended on a higher note. It was a magnificent achievement and certainly one of my most cherished memories.

Perhaps, strangely, one of the lingering memories of that great day was not of our performance in the afternoon but of the All Blacks in the evening. Their manager, Russ Thomas, captain Graham Mourie and all their players were magnanimous and gracious in defeat. They looked for no excuses, offered no complaints and praised us generously for our well-deserved victory. Mind you, they also warned us it would be quite different the following week at Twickenham, and how right they were.

Being the dedicated outfit they are, the All Blacks used every waking moment planning their revenge. They produced a different style and a few crucial changes in personnel for the international seven days later. Their most significant change was to switch Murray Taylor to fly half from centre in place of Eddie Dunn. They also moved Stuart Wilson into the centre and introduced Brian Ford on the wing. They also placed Mourie at the back of the line-out instead of third from the back as he had been at Otley, and with his phenomenal speed he became much more involved in the loose at Twickenham.

While they shrewdly strengthened their side, the new England selectors made the only real mess of their first three years in office. The first name on our team sheet should have been Alan Old, specially as Mike Davis intended to play the same style as the North had done. Incredibly, he was left out in favour of Les Cusworth, a very talented individual but at that stage very much a running fly half. It was an unbelievable decision that was to cost us the match. On the same basis, it was equally irresponsible not to pick Roger Uttley at flank to do exactly the same job he had done so well for the North. Again, Mike Rafter, a player of undoubted international class, was not the style of flanker we needed for that particular game. Rafter would have walked into most international sides during the late seventies, but he was unlucky that he had to live in the shadow of such world-class flankers as Tony Neary and Peter Dixon. His talent was in ample evidence during England's tour to Argentina in 1981 when he enjoyed great success.

At Twickenham, England tried to play the same style as the previous week but without the players capable of doing it. We had a running fly half and, in Nick Preston, a running centre, whereas we needed a kicking fly half and a crash-tackling centre. If nothing else, the selectors learned something about horses for courses. Under Budge Rodgers they never made such a bad selection again. It was all summed up at the press conference when the team was announced. Budge was asked how often the halfbacks, Cusworth and Smith, had played together and how well. He replied that although he had never seen them together, he was assured they had played well as a pair and was confident they would serve England well. In fact, they had never played or even practised together before that day – surely something the selectors should have known. Smith and Old had played together countless times. It was an amazing decision to split them up the day after their greatest triumph together. Since then, Cusworth has made rapid strides and is now an accomplished player, but it was not fair on him to be picked for that match.

Before we had time to settle in, the All Blacks had opened up a 10-point lead, including the only try of the game, scored by Fleming. It was a tense, dour struggle and although Dusty Hare kicked three penalties to narrow the gap to just 1 point, the All Blacks had raised their game dramatically from the previous week and they deserved their victory.

Funnily enough, our pack still played well; if we had picked the right team we might well have won. At the press conference afterwards I shattered the assembled throng of scribblers by confidently stating that from such a humble defeat we were now in a position to build for the Home International Championship and I was in no doubt we would win both the Triple Crown and take the Championship. That comment was greeted with incredulous laughter by the press, but in the end I had the last laugh.

12

The Grand Slam – 1980

One of the most important reasons for England's lack of success in the seventies was the consistently bad selection. Therefore, it is only fair to give the selectors full credit when they did eventually strike gold in 1980. The selection of Phil Blakeway at tight-head prop for the opening game against Ireland in January at Twickenham was critical to our success.

Little had been heard of Phil since he went on the Australian tour in 1975; three years later he had the misfortune to break his neck. He had only played a handful of games for Gloucester when he found himself picked for the Rest team in the final trial. Clint McGregor played tight-head in the England team but he gave away several penalties during the trial when he was caught off-side and that must have counted against him.

Later that evening Mike Davis asked what I would recommend for the front row combination and I suggested switching Fran Cotton to tight-head and bringing in Colin Smart at loose-head. I had not realized the impact Phil Blakeway had had on our scrum in the trial. In the end the selectors kept Fran on the loose side and picked Phil Blakeway for his renowned scrummaging ability at tight-head. Roger Uttley was brought back at flank forward and John Horton replaced Les Cusworth at fly half. He was the ideal fly half to play the kind of controlled, disciplined rugby we had decided to pursue and he had a vital role in the next two months.

We had a full squad training weekend leading up to

the Irish match and Mike Davis concentrated on a few
key areas where he felt we needed most improvement.
Mike also had an uncanny knack of practising the odd
little forward skill with groups of three or four players;
amazingly, the opportunity to use these particular skills
often seemed to crop up in our actual matches. We did
a great deal of support play in small groups and the type
of situations he worked out for us were repeated in all
the internationals.

Maurice Colclough dropped out of the first match
through injury and was replaced by Nigel Horton. That
was to be Nigel's last game of international rugby. He
had hardly played any rugby that season because of a
disagreement with his club side in France. In the circumstances, he had a magnificent game and dominated
the middle of the line-out.

Ireland were favourites for the Championship. They
had won both Tests on their summer tour of Australia
and their new fly half, Ollie Campbell, had emerged as
a deadly accurate goal kicker and talented all-round
footballer. At the Friday training session the day before
the match, I took our pack on one side and told them
exactly what their responsibility was. It was essential for
us to destroy the Irish pack or we would be in big
trouble. If we allowed their forwards to break even, then
Campbell would pin us in our own half with his tactical
kicking and, eventually, if we gave away penalties under
pressure, he would win the game for Ireland.

If we were not on top in the forward battle, then our
backs would be tempted to run the ball in desperation
and this would play right into the Irish hands. They
were the best scavengers and predators in the world and
with a brilliant back row of Slattery, Duggan and
O'Driscoll they could carve our backs to pieces if we
allowed them the freedom to tear round the pitch all
afternoon. I emphasized that the time for messing
around in a half-hearted fashion was over. We had a job
to do and we were going to do it. We had to scrummage
them off the field, drive at them in every line-out, and

completely tie in and commit their loose forwards before spinning the ball out to our backs. We had to keep them under fierce combative pressure throughout the whole match and never give them an opportunity to relax or counterattack. At long last the selectors had given us the pack to carry out this demolition job and if we all played our part we would share in a great victory.

Ireland have always been the greatest spoilers in the world. It was up to us to give them no opportunity to disrupt our backs – we had to drive their forwards back all the time. When in doubt, Steve Smith and John Horton were to keep us going forward with kicks.

We decided to play the game in their half of the field and eliminate all risks in our own half. We were perfectly prepared to believe that Ollie Campbell was a phenomenally accurate goal kicker without requiring any visual proof to that effect at Twickenham that afternoon. If we spent the match camped in their half, we had our own goal-kicking match winner in Dusty Hare.

Our plan of campaign was blissfully simple on paper, but in reality it was no easy task to contain, let alone destroy, the Irish pack. Traditionally, the Irish forwards comprised eight whirlwind terriers and it was a marvellous achievement to tame them that day. We had practised our back-row defence in the fullest possible detail and we were ready for the sniping, ferret-like dashes of Colin Patterson and the bulldozing charges of Duggan and Slattery. At every Irish scrum and in the loose, one player always stood out to mark Patterson – he was their only really dangerous, penetrating runner.

For once, the best laid plans of mice and men actually came off. We tied up the Irish loose forwards by peeling from the line-out, rolling off mauls by unleashing Tony Bond in mid-field. Once their back row and a couple of their backs were buried at the bottom of a ruck or maul, our backs launched their own attacks. Dusty Hare gave us the lead with a penalty early on, but then our concentration lapsed for a period of six minutes midway through the first half and we gave away three penalties just inside our own half. They were all from wide angles but, sure enough, Campbell, with his in-built radar system, slotted the lot to put Ireland 9–3 ahead.

That spurred us into a flurry of activity and we rattled up another 12 points before half time. A prolonged offensive by our pack ended with Smithy darting over from a ruck near the line and when the Irish fullback, Kevin O'Brien, made an error, Mike Slemen swooped on the bouncing ball to score in the corner. Dusty Hare converted both tries. In the second half, he kicked another penalty and converted a try by Scott after more driving forward. We exerted such total domination and command up front that victory was a formality.

The one blemish on an otherwise perfect day was the horrendous injury to Tony Bond twenty minutes from the end of the match. In a tackle on Alistair McKibbin, Tony got an accidental crack on the leg and fell awkwardly to suffer an awful spiral fracture. The bone was sticking right out and it was a terrible sight. He was replaced by Clive Woodward and did not play rugby again for a very long time.

My other minor regret was my failure to score a try near the end. It was the closest that I ever came to scoring in an international; I did not realize I was within a yard of the line when I was tackled by Colin Patterson, the smallest player on the pitch. I should have driven through the tackle and would have definitely scored, but, instead, I turned to give the ball to the supporting players and they were held up by the Irish forwards on the line.

Nevertheless, it had been a good day's work. We had beaten the favourites to win 24–9 and we set off for Paris a fortnight later with our confidence as high as it had ever been since my first cap in 1975. We had a squad session on the Monday evening of that week and this was a popular decision with the players. Often on a Sunday they were stiff or had bumps and bruises and most of them preferred to spend the day with their families. Since 1980 we have always trained on a Monday night in the Midlands and this has been universally well received.

We made two changes for the Paris game – Woodward took over from the injured Bond and Colclough replaced Nigel Horton. At the time, I told the press that we were engaged in a four-lap race and we had now safely negotiated the first lap. There was still a long way to go. Our recent record in Paris made haunting reading, but the French selectors had done us an enormous favour by picking a very strange pack. Blakeway had helped us crucify the Irish scrummage and, knowing this, the French astonished everyone by picking at loose-head prop a player who had previously specialized at lock or No. 8. It was a crazy thing to do and, needless to say, after eighty minutes locked in mortal combat with Blakeway, Patrick Salas was duly murdered and never played for France again. We hopelessly outscrummaged them. Even during a brief period when Uttley was off the field having a cut stitched, we still pushed them back with only seven forwards.

Their locks, Maleig and Duhard, were small men and not recognized jumpers. This allowed us to dominate the line-out and from this platform we got on top in the loose, denying their gifted backs much of the ball, which was exactly what we had intended in our pre-match preparations. That was just as well because, after two days of snow and slush, the sun shone on the Saturday and there was the inevitable risk that the French would cut loose at any time and produce some of the flowing champagne rugby for which they are justifiably famous.

They started with a bang when Rives scored a try in the second minute of the game. Hare kicked a penalty for us but then Fran Cotton gave one away which Caussade kicked. Robert Paparemborde, who was a great tight-head prop, kept boring in on our hooker, Peter Wheeler, and deliberately collapsing the scrum. To encourage Paparemborde to stop this illegal manoeuvre, Fran took the law into his own hands. The referee, Clive Norling, awarded France a penalty, but it took Fran's revenge to convince Paparemborde to play by the rules for the rest of the match.

Our pack reproduced the same repetitive, driving, closequarter play that had ripped the heart out of the Irish and it had the same pulverizing effect on the French. With our forwards churning back such quality possession of the highest order, Preston and Carleton ran in two tries before half time. Hare converted one and John Horton dropped a goal after receiving a controlled ball from the seven-man scrum while Uttley was off the field. That scrum summed it all up. The huge technical deficiencies of Salas had been fully exposed and exploited, and the French were in a hopeless, helpless position. Horton dropped another goal at the start of the second half and I begged our players not to let the French off the hook – they were at their most dangerous when they were on the rack; they would cut loose if they were given any breathing space at all. We tried desperately to increase our tempo but the French, after absorbing relentless pressure for seventy minutes, dredged up the energy to win some ball late on and, with nothing to lose, they engineered some lovely, sweeping handling movements which stretched us to the limit.

Averous eventually scored in the corner and Caussade converted to cut our lead to 4 points. As the conversion was being taken I told the team that it was ridiculous to dominate a match for seventy minutes and then throw it all away, and I asked everyone to redouble his efforts. Because of our excellent defensive organization and new-found confidence and belief in our own ability, we were able to cling on to our lead, aided by some good tackling.

It was our first win at Parc des Princes Stadium and our first win in France for sixteen years. There were fantastic scenes of rejoicing in the dressing room as we realized we were still in the lead after two laps of our race and were halfway to our Grand Slam.

Half an hour later I went out on to the pitch to be interviewed by Bill McLaren for television. Thousands of English supporters were still there wallowing in general euphoria. For twenty minutes on either side of half time our patient supporters had witnessed English rugby at its very best as we swept France aside and took complete control. It was an afternoon to savour; the evening was not too bad either.

We went with the French players to the Moulin Rouge, where we lapped up the extravagant floor show, and then went on to one or two night clubs where some serious gargling was done. I vaguely recall eating a meal in a small bistro at about six o'clock in the morning with Dusty Hare, Maurice Colclough and a couple of French players, before crawling and staggering back to the hotel for breakfast. It was dawn when we arrived back in time to see the main party preparing to depart for the airport. I had arranged to spend the day in Paris and after seeing the bus off, I retired to bed for an hour's kip.

When Hilary met me late that night at Manchester Airport, I was still in a very fragile state but was able to look back with tremendous satisfaction on a great victory the day before. I can still conjure up in my mind's eye the emotional scenes in the dressing room and the unashamed joy of our legion of long-suffering English fans whom we encountered from time to time during the twenty-four pulsating hours after the final whistle.

The next fortnight was not one of the most pleasant episodes in player–press relationships. The build-up to the England–Wales match was a sordid, distasteful affair, sparked off by some irresponsible comments in some sections of the press.

It all began with reports in various papers which claimed that Fran Cotton had said that if Graham Price, the Welsh tight-head prop, tried any nonsense in the set scrums, then he would be prepared to sort him out. These alleged comments by Fran were so ridiculous and out of character that it was no surprise when Fran denied them, but it unfortunately fuelled plenty of controversy in Wales. Fran and Pricey were old campaigners who had played a lot of rugby together and had great mutual respect for each other, and neither would have had anything to do with disreputable, cheap journalism. Once these reports appeared, however, the damage was done and the popular press in both countries began to build up the match into a personal battle of player against player – in which Geoff Wheel and I figured fairly prominently – and a grand national confrontation of country against country. This sort of media coverage is quite unnecessary in an amateur game; sadly, it happens all too frequently in South Africa and New Zealand where any suspected personal animosities are stirred up to encourage further antagonism and strife.

With players of both countries reading pages of garbage in the two weeks leading up to the Twickenham match, it was understandable that relations were a shade frosty. Inevitably some added needle would appear on the field of play. A major share of the blame for what happened during the game can be apportioned to the press. There was a steel strike in Wales at the time and part of the propaganda in some papers revolved round the national pride of the hard-pressed, down-trodden, Welsh working class fighting for their rights against the well-to-do, toffee-nosed English. It was incredible bunkum but it left its mark and scarred some minds.

One article referred to the Cardiff and England No. 8 John Scott, who played his club rugby in the Principality. It was suggested that because he was about to play for England against Wales, he was going to show everyone he was the toughest and roughest player of them all.

The Welsh papers mentioned that Wales had only lost once to England in the previous sixteen years and that was in 1974 when, they alleged, the referee, John West, had given a bad decision which deprived Wales of the victory they deserved. Now here was a chance for revenge against a mediocre English side who were playing dull, negative rugby. This verbal warfare reached fever pitch towards the end of the second week. At our training sessions on the Thursday and Friday prior to the game, I had to spend most of my time cooling our lads down rather than trying to psyche them up. I persuaded them that we were the better footballers and it would go against us if we became embroiled in a brawl all afternoon.

Forty-eight hours before the game, the team was actually strengthened by the greater physical presence of Paul Dodge. He replaced Nick Preston who dropped out because of injury.

Also on the Thursday there was a scare about Phil Blakeway, who had done so much to help us win the first two matches. He had been kicked on the ribs during the French game and was in some pain after the Thursday practice. Our physiotherapist, Don Gatherer, thought he had broken his ribs, so our team doctor Leon Walkden took him to hospital for an x-ray, which was negative. Phil insisted on playing and asked for pain-killing injections just before the match. It was later discovered that his ribs were indeed broken and that accounts for the fact that he was not quite such a potent force in the Welsh match. He must have been in considerable pain throughout, despite the injections.

I had little idea of what was going to happen in the first twenty minutes of the match. At the first line-out there was a bit of a scuffle, with elbows, arms and bodies going in every direction. The opening exchanges were conducted in an unreal atmosphere and the crowd were baying as if they were at a bull fight or watching the Roman gladiators against the Christians. Dusty Hare was blatantly late tackled early on and someone had a go at Mike Slemen and Clive Woodward. The scrums were going down with a frightening ferocity as the respective front rows charged at each other. There was no quarter asked or given and the match turned out to be one of the roughest and most abrasive I can ever remember.

Many of the niggly comments throughout the game were not really worthy of the people who made them.

For example, at almost every line-out, Geoff Wheel made some sort of cryptic comment to me, usually along the following lines: 'You think you're going to be captain of the Lions, do you? Do you think you'll captain the Lions, then? You think you're going to win today, do you?' He really need not have wasted his breath. He would have been better using all his energy jumping for the ball. I never replied, but just burst my gut trying to win every line-out. A few scuffles broke out between players in that opening spell and after ten minutes the referee, David Burnett, took Jeff Squire and myself on one side and told us to tell our teams that the next person to commit an act of foul play would be sent off. I asked the referee if I could have a minute to talk to my team and he agreed. I gathered everyone together and told them that the next person to throw a punch or do anything silly would be sent off for certain. I repeated what I had said in the changing room – that we would win if we concentrated on playing rugby. I warned them that the next person to indulge in any form of rough play would have to be a lunatic. A few minutes later, Paul Ringer openly committed a late and dangerous tackle on John Horton after the fly half had kicked ahead. Ringer was quite rightly sent off.

I would defend Ringer in so far as his tackle was not, by a long way, the dirtiest tackle I've seen on a rugby pitch, but knowing the attitude of the referee, which had been clearly and forcibly relayed by the two captains to all the players, his act was one of the utmost, unbelievable folly. That type of play may or may not have been his natural game, but to have tackled late and dangerously moments after a general final warning was, I thought, the height of stupidity and the action of a fool. I can honestly say, with my hand on my heart, that if any of the English team had behaved with similar irresponsible indiscipline, I would have felt exactly the same and defended the referee completely. The game can do without that sort of incident. It did nothing for international rugby, for Wales or, of course, for Paul Ringer.

His controversial career ended in humiliating ignominy and he had no one to blame but himself. I find it a tiny bit disappointing that the admirable Max Boyce, who has given such enormous pleasure to rugby folk everywhere, myself included, should have felt the need to write a song depicting the hapless Ringer as a martyr.

With sixty-five minutes left, I told our team that we could never hold our heads high again if we lost to fourteen men. Had Ringer not been sent off, Wales would probably have won. The biggest cross he will have to bear for the rest of his life is the fact that he let down fourteen team mates, 25,000 supporters at the game, and a whole passionate nation glued to the television set. In fact, Hare kicked the penalty which we were awarded for the Ringer incident and, in the end, those points made the difference between the two teams.

From the restart after that penalty, Wales attacked and scored from some bad scrummage ball on our line. We heeled, but were partially wheeled, and when the ball squirted out the side, Jeff Squire scored.

They held that 4–3 lead until half time at which point we lost Roger Uttley, who received an awful boot on the face from one of the Welsh forwards who claimed afterwards that the injury was entirely accidental as, at the time, he was trying to kick the ball. That's as maybe, but he split Uttley's nose wide open and there was blood everywhere.

After the interval the game settled down and I think both sides were a bit inhibited. Play was still fiercely physical and bruisingly hard but I was not aware of any overtly dirty play. A quarter of an hour from the end, we went ahead with a second penalty from Dusty Hare and I exhorted our team to hang on until the final whistle. Wales could have had the match sewn up if their goal kickers had been in form, but Gareth Davies, Allan Martin and Steve Fenwick all missed kicks, any one of which would have won them the match.

However, Wales played remarkably well with only fourteen men and looked to have won the game with a try three minutes from the end which put them 8–6 ahead. I had given instructions to Smithy and John Horton to bang the ball down into the Welsh half every time they got it towards the end. But Smithy had a kick charged down by Alan Phillips near the halfway line. Wales broke through and Elgan Rees crossed in the corner for a try. If he had had his wits about him, he would have run towards the posts, which he certainly could have done, and that would have made the conversion simple and given Wales a 4-point lead. As it was, Davies missed the kick and we only trailed 8–6.

Smithy was squatting on his haunches near the touch line looking dejected. I wandered across to him, looked him straight in the eyes and told him I knew exactly how he felt and he was not to worry about it. As the conversion was being taken I pointed out that the final whistle had not yet gone and there was still time to produce a miracle. He nodded but was choking back tears at the same time.

We kicked off to restart the match and the ball was scrambled into touch by Wales. I called for a two-man line-out on the simple premise that we were more likely to win quick clean possession that way, and John Scott palmed to Smithy. He passed to me at about ankle height, which any self-respecting lock forward should have knocked on. I desperately did not want to let Smithy or the team down in what was probably our last attack. Remembering the one thing I learned during my years as a schoolboy fly half, I kept my eyes riveted on the ball and bent right down on the run to scoop it up safely. I slipped the ball to Paul Dodge, who set up a ruck wide out near the touch line on the right-hand side of the field. Terry Holmes was penalized for going over the top and we had a penalty to win the match.

I walked over to Dusty Hare, looked at him and gave him the ball. I wanted to wish him luck but I couldn't summon up the strength to utter a word. For the first time on a rugby field, I actually looked up at the heavens and prayed for divine intervention. As Dusty lined up the ball, I looked up into the stand where I knew Hilary was sitting and spotted her in a white coat. She was looking away, unable to stand the strain. Dusty's wife Lesley was wilting under the tension as well. I closed my eyes as Dusty ran up and, as I heard him make contact, I looked up to see the ball soaring between the posts through a gathering crescendo of cheering.

As we ran back I implored the boys not to relax until the final whistle which mercifully followed very quickly. The first person to shake my hand afterwards was Graham Price who offered his congratulations and said there was no ill feeling at all between us. I then shook hands with Geoff Wheel and we thanked each other for the game.

There were fantastic scenes in the dressing room although it partly resembled a busy casualty department on a Saturday night with a few players spilling blood. I had a few stitches myself and then went round my team to thank everyone personally. They had shown a lot of character in a disgraceful game of rugby which had been an appalling advertisement for the sport. Nevertheless, for once luck had been on our side. It was wonderful to think that the third lap of the race was over and we only had to gear ourselves up for one final fling.

People have often reminded me that it takes two to tango, but I want to make it clear that the over-vigorous and over-enthusiastic play at the outset came fairly and squarely from the Welsh. Having said that, I do not claim for a moment that we were innocent angels throughout the game. Once the standard had been set, the English players showed they were quite prepared to look after themselves. But I want to emphasize that at no stage in any of our preparations was any mention of a rough, physical approach ever made by me, by Mike Davis, by Budge Rodgers or by any of the players. We did not want a dirty game, we had not planned for one and were thoroughly ashamed afterwards that we had been involved in one. Ten minutes after the end of the match, I went into the Welsh dressing room to try to diffuse the situation and talked to almost all the Welsh team. I said to Jeff Squire that we all knew each other so well; we had toured together in the past and would tour together in the future. I thought it best to admit we had all made a mess that afternoon; we should wipe the slate clean and start all over again.

After the press conference, which was handled as delicately as possible, the senior vice-president of the RFU, John Kendall-Carpenter, told me the crowd were calling for me out on the pitch. He suggested I make a brief appearance in the committee box to acknowledge them. When I got there I was flabbergasted at the amazing scene in front of me. Thousands of delirious, almost hysterical, supporters were chanting my name and when I waved and gave them the thumbs-up sign they screamed and cheered their approval. They had patiently waited a good many years to indulge themselves in such celebrations and I was really delighted that at last we had given our followers something to cheer about. Vast numbers of the emotionally charged crowd were still in the ground long after the final whistle had gone, and a buoyant Hilary had to be helped to the team coach by two policemen.

At the dinner I made a point of seeking out Paul Ringer to apologize for what had happened and suggest that bygones be bygones. I said that he must be feeling depressed but it would only be worse if he sulked on his own and the best thing to do was to join in everything that evening.

I had a pleasant surprise after the dinner. The British Lions were due to leave on a major tour of South Africa in May and the team was expected to be announced at the end of March. The manager, Syd Miller, took me aside that night and asked me if I would accept the captaincy of the Lions. I said that I would love to and it was all settled there and then. For the next month I told no one apart from Hilary – not even my parents – although I was tempted to approach Geoff Wheel around midnight and tell him the answer to the question he had been boring me to death with all through the game during the afternoon!

In the week after the Welsh match I admitted to the media that the game had done rugby a lot of harm and that the English team were not proud of their part in it. However, that was history now and we were looking forward to the future and the possibility of a first Grand Slam since 1957.

The Wales–Scotland match two weeks later was a very timid affair by comparison, partly because, to their eternal credit, the Welsh selectors and the Welsh rugby hierarchy had read their team the riot act after the Twickenham exhibition. Scotland were comfortably beaten and this gave our confidence a boost.

The month between the Welsh match and the Scottish game seemed an interminably long time, but after our weekend squad session in the middle of it, the evening session on the Monday six days before the game, plus the usual Thursday and Friday practice sessions immediately prior to the game, we knew that no England side had ever been better prepared for such an important match.

I received several hundred letters and telegrams wishing us luck and was able to impress the team during the final build-up with the huge number of well-wishers who were relying on us. I had, incidentally, also received many aggressive letters from Wales attacking the English team and our recent performances. The atmosphere in the ground was fantastic. Since we had arrived in Edinburgh on the Thursday, the town had been buzzing in anticipation. Droves of English fans swept up and down Princes Street and it was the most emotional and passionate prelude to a game that I can recall. Infuriatingly, one of my cousins had, quite unwittingly, decided to get married that particular Saturday and my parents felt duty bound to attend the wedding. This meant that, having followed me regularly from those not so palmy days in the Fylde sixth team right through all the good times as well as all the bad, my father was destined to miss my finest hour. That was my only regret that day. On the morning of the match I hunted for a shop which could sell me a tankard and have it inscribed within an hour, because that was the day that Tony Neary became England's most capped player in history and the team wanted to make him a presentation after the match.

On the Saturday morning, Mike Davis went over the match plan in meticulous detail, covering an enormous number of little points but, basically, our tactics were simple. We had to destroy the Scottish pack to deprive the likes of Rutherford, Renwick, Johnston and Irvine any attacking opportunities from quick loose ball. We would repeat the job we had done on Ireland and run good second-phase possession when the Scottish back row had been otherwise engaged by our forwards and rendered, temporarily at least, *hors de combat*. We wanted to win the Triple Crown, the Championship and the Grand Slam, but we also wanted to do it in style. We succeeded beyond our wildest dreams.

In the dressing room Mike Davis gave a final word of encouragement and then I got all the players together for the last reminder of the task we faced. We were eighty minutes away from glory and each and every one of us had a vital role to play to ensure we achieved our destiny. We knew we were the better side, we were confident but not arrogant, and we appreciated that we needed every ounce of energy and concentration to assert our superiority and collect the pot of gold which was waiting at the end of the rainbow. Our team photograph before the match summed it all up. The expression on every face told the story and it was clear from our collective determination and commitment, we were not going to be denied our ultimate prize.

The record book shows that we annihilated Scotland in the first half and duly lead 19–3 at half time. With our pack rampant we met only modest resistance and a fine run by Clive Woodward led to our first try which was scored by John Carleton. Woodward then cut out the early work for a try by Mike Slemen on the other wing before Carleton scored again after being set up by Scott and Smith. Hare converted the first two tries and kicked a penalty to put us almost out of reach.

Midway through the second half we had increased our lead to 23–6 with another try from Steve Smith and a second penalty by Hare. All Scotland had managed were two penalties by Andy Irvine, but then they staged a dramatic recovery as they began to win a bit of ball for the first time in the match and they opened out from every conceivable position.

They delighted the capacity crowd of 75,000 with some breathtaking running and were rewarded with two tries by Alan Tomes and John Rutherford, both converted by Irvine. In the midst of this hectic, frenetic rally, Dusty Hare kicked another penalty for us and John Carleton helped himself to his third try. We clung on to our 30–18 lead during a thrilling last ten minutes in which I was aching to hear the final whistle. Suddenly, it went and, lo and behold, we were Champions. We had done the lot. We had scored our highest ever total against Scotland, retained the Calcutta Cup, won the Championship, collected our first Triple Crown for twenty years and completed the Grand Slam for the first time since 1957.

It was odd that when the final whistle blew I found myself at that precise moment surrounded by the three guys who had been through all the bad times with me and who would particularly cherish the memories of that unforgettable season. Peter Wheeler, Fran Cotton, Tony Neary and I stood on the pitch together and, glowing with English pride, we hugged each other triumphantly. In a spontaneous gesture, Fran and Peter lifted me onto their shoulders and chaired me off the pitch. Our dressing room was a scene of undiluted jubilation as everyone hugged each other in the overwhelming euphoria of the occasion.

I went to the Scottish dressing room to thank them for a wonderfully entertaining game which produced seven cracking tries and then returned to our own celebrations. I called for some hush while I thanked the selectors, the players and the reserves for the tremendous effort all year and I presented Tony Neary with the tankard to mark his record forty-third, and as it so happened, his last cap. There was no more appropriate way for this great player to end his distinguished career. I did a quick interview for BBC television and as I battled my way back to our changing room through a throng of exultant English supporters, someone thrust a beautiful pure wool sweater into my hand. When I got back to the relative safety of our team room, I looked at the sweater and saw it had the bright red rose of England and a huge emblem which read: GRAND SLAM CHAMPIONS – 1980. It was somewhat precocious but one of the boys said, 'Put it on.' 'No,' I replied, 'I'm not going to wear it. Remember the words of John Burgess – "always show humility and grace both in defeat and in victory".'

The team climbed aboard the coach and at that moment it was probably the happiest place on earth. The general feeling was one of excitement and relief. When we reached our hotel it was bustling with activity. I was delighted to be greeted by members of the Fylde Rugby Club. Fylde had played against Gala in Scotland that morning and were there to share our triumph.

The team were mobbed all night by ecstatic supporters and the champagne flowed freely until the early hours of the morning. At one stage early in the evening though, Fran, Nero and I slipped away to a bar for a quiet drink. There we recalled the black days of 1976 when we lost every game and no one wanted to know us. We also talked about the ups and downs in between. We all savoured that day because we knew it was a once-in-a-lifetime experience – 'Like the snow upon the river, a moment white then gone for ever'.

I have one other memory of that glorious afternoon. Only the fifteen England players who took part will ever really know what it felt like when the final whistle went.

Only they will ever be able to understand it fully. All the press, who had written millions of cutting, damning words about English rugby between 1957 and 1980, all the former England international players, all the spectators, all the experts and all the ordinary punters could only guess what that moment of ecstasy actually felt like. I was one of the fifteen and I shall never forget it. Alan Tomes came up to me in the tunnel and asked to swap jerseys with me. In the past I had always exchanged my jersey with my opponent, but on this special occasion I declined as politely as I could. I explained that I had waited all my life for that one moment of triumph and I doubted I would ever be fortunate enough to enjoy a repeat performance. I wanted to keep and treasure that particular jersey with its unique memories and associations until the day I died. I wanted it, bespattered with mud as it was, stuck on my study wall for ever as a perpetual reminder of 15 March 1980. Alan could see that I was glowing with pride and, slapping me on the back, he smiled. He knew exactly what I meant and how I felt.

13

Lions in South Africa – 1980

After the Calcutta Cup match, we had a champagne celebration at our hotel followed by the dinner, but for a lot of the players their minds were on other things. The British Lions party was due to be finalized the following day and I spent a few minutes at the dinner talking to the Lions manager, Syd Miller.

I was not officially involved in selection, but Syd did discuss the loose-head props with me. Budge Rogers, the England representative on the Lions selection, felt that Fran Cotton no longer relished the physical side of the game and Budge did not feel he should go on the tour. I thought that was complete nonsense and told Syd that I definitely felt Fran should be picked. On the Sunday morning I phoned Budge to tell him my point of view, and he said that if I felt that strongly about it, then he would support Fran's selection.

Unlike the 1977 trip to New Zealand, we had an excellent management in Syd Miller and Noel Murphy. Syd was a strong man with a powerful personality who knew the demands, problems and pitfalls of a South African tour inside out. He had toured there with the Lions previously, both as a player and as a coach, and he was clearly the best man for the job. Noel Murphy was the senior international coach in Britain at the time and he had been responsible for Ireland's highly successful tour to Australia the previous summer when Ireland won both internationals.

I thought it was unfair to criticize the choice of Syd

and Noel just because they were both Irish, as nationality really does not matter once the party arrives in a foreign country. The more significant criticism concerned the selection of three forwards to run the tour. In Syd Miller, Noel Murphy and myself, the ruling triumvirate comprised a prop, a flanker and a lock. The only senior and experienced back on the trip was Andy Irvine and he did not join the party until after the first Test.

In future I think care should be taken to achieve a sensible blend among the management hierarchy, although, having said that, I believe the most important single aspect is to ensure that the coach and the captain get on well together and are on the same wave-length, irrespective of their specialized positions.

On the Monday morning after the Calcutta Cup match, Noel Murphy rang me from Edinburgh with the names of the touring party and on the whole I was pretty pleased with the job the selectors had done. I was surprised and disappointed that no place had been found for Dusty Hare at fullback, Paul Dodge in the centre, Geoff Wheel at lock and John Scott at No. 8. The glaring weakness was at flank forward where we desperately needed either Fergus Slattery or Tony Neary. Both were unavailable and there were no real alternatives of the same calibre. The combination of blistering speed, great experience, and the ability to destroy the opposition mid-field with oppressive pressure is given to few players. Rob Louw showed that he had it in all four Tests for South Africa, but we had no comparable forward in our party.

The selectors knew the need for a tearaway flanker on the hard grounds in South Africa and, deprived of Slattery and Neary, they chose Stuart Lane of Cardiff and Wales. What sort of a job Lane would have done is open to conjecture, but he was injured in the second minute of the first match and took no further part in the tour. He was sorely missed. We were left with a back row full of strength and physical presence but lacking in genuine pace to the breakdown. We survived in the provincial matches but were shown up by Rob Louw in the Tests. He scored the opening try in each of the first two Tests and was an outstanding support player round the field.

Our injury problems actually began before the opening match. When we assembled in London prior to flying from Heathrow, Andy Irvine dropped out with a pulled hamstring which he had injured playing in the Cathay Pacific World Sevens in Hong Kong. The Cathay Pacific Tournament is undoubtedly the best sevens competition in the world, but one must question the wisdom of playing in it so near the beginning of a Lions tour. Had we spent a week training at Eastbourne before departing for South Africa as usual, Andy might have recovered in time, but we decided to avoid any possibility of political demonstrations by assembling in London less than twenty-four hours before our departure. Funnily enough, I did not receive a single letter or telegram from anyone trying to persuade me not to go to South Africa, whereas I did receive several hundred letters urging me to go and wishing me luck.

Elgan Rees was drafted into the side at the last moment, partly, I think, because he was already at Heathrow preparing to leave with Wales on a tour to America. I should have much preferred Peter Squires as replacement wing for Irvine as I rated him a better footballer than Rees and he was also an excellent rugby tourist.

The strength of the tour manager was forcibly expressed before we flew from London. At dinner prior to departure several of the players ordered wine with their meal but made themselves extremely scarce when it came to paying the bill. At the first team meeting, Syd Miller announced that the tallest man in the room would pay the wine bill and it would be up to him to find out who the various debtors were and to extract money from them. Justice was seen to be done when it became clear that the tallest player was Allan Martin. His team-mates reckoned that it was just about his turn to pay for a round anyway. Poor Allan spent the first couple of weeks of the tour trying to recoup his money, but Syd's action

Right: In the committee box, acknowledging the cheers of our jubilant supporters after beating Wales

1980 Grand Slam. *Back row (left to right):* S. G. B. Mills, J.-P. Bonnet (France referee), W. H. Hare, P. W. Dodge, R. M. Uttley, M. J. Colclough, J. P. Scott, F. E. Cotton, A. Neary, M. Keyworth, G. A. F. Sargent, F. Palmade (France, touch judge). *Middle row:* G. Chevrier (France, touch judge), P. J. Wheeler, C. R. Woodward, M. A. C. Slemen, W. B. B., S. J. Smith, J. Carleton, P. J. Blakeway. *Front row:* A. G. B. Old, J. A. Palmer, I. G. Peck, J. P. Horton

Left: England coach Mike Davis who, with Budge Rogers, was the architect of our success

Below: Dusty Hare kicks the winning penalty in injury time against Wales

Bottom: On the attack for England against Scotland in the final leg of the Grand Slam

Top: Willie John McBride of Ireland *Bottom:* Graham Mourie of New Zealand

Fergus Slattery of Ireland

Gordon Brown of Scotland

Jean-Pierre Rives of France

Phil Bennett of Wales

Below: Who cares if the whistle has gone!

Right: With the mascot before the Transvaal match in Johannesburg in 1980

Just don't miss touch, Andy

Left: Noel Murphy hits the Coca-Cola yet again

Below: Springbok captain Morne du Plessis holds my hand high after our victory in the final Test. We won the match – they won the series

Below: When our scrum half asked for protection, we did our best to oblige

Have you heard the one about. . .? 'Is it true, Bill, that Mother has invited you round to the house for lunch?'

Hilary and I slipping in our wedding between matches

With my OBE at Buckingham Palace, flanked by Hilary and my parents

Above: Being introduced to HRH Queen Elizabeth before the Welsh Centenary Match at Cardiff in 1980

Below: My only try at international level – England and Wales against Scotland and Ireland at Cardiff in 1980

did let the whole party know that he was going to stand no nonsense.

We arrived in Johannesburg on a Sunday morning and that afternoon Noel Murphy decided to hold a training session. As befits an Irishman, he got off to a hilarious start with his opening sentence as coach at the warm-up. 'To do this exercise,' he said, 'it's best to spread out in a bunch.' The Irish players had no difficulty in following such precise instructions, but the rest of us were a little puzzled!

We trained hard all week and a fine edge was put on our fitness, but we received another setback when David Richards learned his father had died; he returned home for a week to attend the funeral. In this first week Ollie Campbell strained a hamstring practising his goal kicking, which left us with two mid-field players unavailable for the first game against Eastern Province in Port Elizabeth.

We accepted these hiccups without too much alarm but at that point we had no idea how the entire tour was going to be ruined by an unprecedented casualty list, which, more than any other single factor, caused us to struggle and lose the Test series. We did remarkably well to win all fourteen provincial games, given our overall injury problems, but the inevitable disruptive effect they had torpedoed any hope of building up a rhythm and a momentum and even frustrated our attempts to settle a Wednesday and a Saturday team quickly.

This had been our intention at the outset and was one of the lessons I had learned in New Zealand in 1977. Sadly, it proved impractical. Our plight was best exemplified by the fact that we used ten completely different combinations at halfback in the first fourteen matches. Depending mainly on injuries and availability we permed four fly halves – Gareth Davies, Ollie Campbell, Tony Ward and David Richards – with three scrum halves – Terry Holmes, Colin Patterson and John Robbie. Ideally, our first-choice halfbacks should have played together seven times by the mid point of the tour but, in fact, by that stage the best we had managed was four different sets of halves who had each managed two games together. To put this all in perspective, suffice to say that during the 1971 Lions tour, Barry John and Gareth Edwards played fourteen matches in harness; our most commonly used partnership was Campbell and Robbie, who were able to complete three games together by the end of the tour.

Our catalogue of disasters makes amazing reading. We lost Andy Irvine and David Richards, both temporarily, before the first match. In that game, Stuart Lane was ruled out of the tour after two minutes with torn knee ligaments and Gareth Davies injured his shoulder before half time and was out of action for a month. In the second game, Phil Blakeway suffered a recurrence of the rib injury which had troubled him at the end of the domestic season and he took no further part in the tour. So great was the dearth of tight-head props in Britain that we chose as his replacement the Bridgend loose-head Ian Stevens, who had a fair amount of experience at tight-head. Gareth Williams replaced Stuart Lane but, in retrospect, we would have been a lot better off with a grafting forward like Mike Rafter.

Perhaps the most serious blow of all was losing Fran Cotton in the sixth match of the tour which was against the South African Federation team, and immediately before the first Test. Fran was suffering from a condition called pericarditis, which in layman's terms means he had inflammation of the covering of his heart. It was one of the very rare occasions during the tour on which I watched a match. I was sitting beside Syd and Noel, and as soon as Fran came off the field ten minutes before half time I told Syd I was worried and rushed off to be with Fran. He had been suffering from a virus infection which had forced him to drop out of the match against Orange Free State the previous Saturday and clearly had not fully recovered from the effects. But the way he was clutching his heart as he was led off the field looked ominous and I honestly thought that he had had a heart attack.

I ran to the changing room and saw our own doctor, Jack Matthews, who was a valuable member of the touring party, and the doctor from Stellenbosch, who was also examining him. Fran showed all the symptoms of having a heart attack. He was taken straightaway to hospital and I went with him, missing the last hour of the match. He underwent a series of tests with electrodes but seemed to be reasonably comfortable. Once I was sure he was in no immediate danger, I returned briefly to the after-match reception. I found Syd and told him the situation. I wanted to go straight back to the hospital and it was agreed that Derek Quinnell would make the captain's speech at the reception. At the hospital in Stellenbosch I checked the latest report on Fran before trying to phone his wife, Pat, in England. The doctors were not sure if he had had a heart attack but I wanted her to hear from me that he was in good spirits and in no danger rather than reading anything alarming in the morning papers. I phoned from my hotel room, doing my best to put her mind at ease. 'Hello, Pat. It's Bill phoning from Cape Town.' 'Oh, my God!' she exclaimed. 'What's happened to Fran? Is he all right?' I gave her a watered-down version of the story, told her not to worry and promised to ring her again in the morning with further news. Fran was transferred the next day to the famous Groote Schur Hospital in Cape Town, where Dr Christiaan Barnard carries out his operations, and, thankfully, he was perfectly okay, having been found not to have had a heart attack after all, but to be suffering instead from pericarditis, a much less serious condition.

We still felt it was probably the end of Fran's rugby career and knew he would not play again on the tour. Our tremendous admiration and affection for him was summed up in one sentence by Peter Wheeler. Dr Barnard had visited Fran in the Groote Schur and jokingly had offered to take him upstairs and give him a new heart which he could choose himself. Peter Wheeler pointed out that there was no heart in the world big enough to replace the one inside Fran Cotton.

Losing Fran was a bitter setback and I had more bad news the next day. Mike Slemen came to my room and told me he had decided to return home because his wife, Eileen, was having a very difficult time. Their young son, Richard, was desperately missing his father and couldn't sleep at night. This meant that Eileen was awake most of the night and as she was pregnant, she was feeling very run down. I fully appreciated the problem with which Mike was confronted and sympathized with him. He wanted to leave at once but I asked him to wait until the weekend and play in the first Test, to which he agreed. This meant that by the seventh game of the tour we had lost the services of Stuart Lane, Phil Blakeway, Fran Cotton and Mike Slemen, apart from a dozen other players who had missed one or two matches through injury.

I knew from the beginning what our strongest pack was and had hoped to play them in all the Saturday matches throughout the tour. It read: Cotton, Wheeler and Price, myself, Colclough or Martin, Squire, Quinnell and Lane. Three of those dropped out injured before the first Test. Slemen would have been in my Saturday side for certain and four more obvious Test players were ruled out of the tour within a week on either side of the second Test. In the week leading up to that match we lost David Richards against Transvaal with a dislocated shoulder which ended his safari, and Terry Holmes, who had earlier dislocated a shoulder, injured his knee ligaments against Eastern Transvaal and had to return home. Gareth Davies, who also suffered a bad shoulder injury in the opening game of the tour, tore his knee ligaments badly during the second Test and that ended his contribution just as he was beginning to inject some confidence, assurance and tactical direction to our back play.

Thus, seven of our likely Test side were all on their

way home by the middle of June and in the very next game against the Junior Springboks in Johannesburg Rodney O'Donnell, our fullback in the first Test, broke his neck. If John O'Driscoll had not been on the pitch to supervise his removal from the place of the injury, he may well have been completely paralysed for life, or worse. John insisted that nobody touch or try to move him until expert medical help arrived. Happily, Rodney has made a complete recovery, although he will never play rugby again. As the most superstitious member of our party, he was able to explain afterwards why he had tempted fate that day. Among his little superstitions were numbered such idiosyncrasies as always coming out of his house backwards, and always feeling compelled to straighten any picture on the wall of his hotel room if it was slightly crooked. He had a set routine for getting in and out of bed and was extremely wary of the numbers 7 and 13. On the day of the Junior Springboks match his size 32 shorts were dirty and Noel Murphy insisted that he borrow a clean pair. The only pair he could find were size 34 – 3 plus 4 makes 7 – and he wore them knowing something awful would probably happen.

By the end of the tour Colin Patterson had also seen his rugby career disintegrate when he received a horrendous knee injury against Griqualand West. This added up to nine players out of the original thirty who failed to complete the tour. We sent for eight replacements during the course of our two-month trip – more than twice as many replacements as had previously been required on a Lions tour. We also had many other less serious injuries which nevertheless plagued us and I still believe we did remarkably well when everything is taken into account.

We won our first six games up to the first Test, but even in the middle of Saturday morning we did not know who would play fly half in the Test. Ollie Campbell was out injured, which left us Gareth Davies, who had almost recovered from his troublesome shoulder injury but had not played for three weeks, David Richards, who was first-choice centre but could conceivably switch to fly half, and Tony Ward, who had flown out to join the party that week but had only played one match in almost two months. We chose Ward, who justified our faith by kicking five penalties and a drop goal. With a try by Graham Price, we scored 22 points but were still beaten by 4 points. Considering that South Africa ran in five tries to our one, we could hardly claim we were unlucky to lose.

Our plan of campaign was forced on us by our spate of injuries and our fear that the South African loose forwards would be faster round the pitch. We decided to keep the match fairly tight and rely on the kicking of Tony Ward to keep us going forward. We had a good attacking threequarter line but it seemed safer to try to dominate up front and play to our pack. The one suspect defensive player in their line-up was Germishuys on the left wing and Syd urged us to concentrate on his poor hands in the first half. Apparently he had been a disaster in the second Test against the Lions in 1974 and Tony Ward pumped a succession of high kicks at him to try to unnerve him. He caught the lot and either returned them with interest or launched counterattacks, putting us under unnecessary pressure either way. The Springboks employed similar tactics, hoping that towering kicks would unsettle O'Donnell at fullback, but he dealt with them bravely and safely even though he did not have the speed to run out of defence or the length of punt to drive South Africa back very far.

The Springboks had been fortunate to have had a warm-up series against South America shortly before we arrived and in those matches a terrific fullback called Gysie Pienaar emerged. He was destined to play a significant part in our downfall and but for the visit of the South Americans, he may well not have been considered. He was the architect of the first try in the Cape Town Test. With O'Donnell lying deep to deal with the monstrous kicking of Naas Botha, Pienaar joined the line and popped a little chip kick into no-man's-land, which covered a large area. South Africa regained possession and the fleet-footed Rob Louw scored. Botha converted.

Two more costly defensive errors led to more tries from Willie du Plessis and Van Heerden and with Botha adding one conversion, we trailed 16–9 at the interval, Ward having kicked three penalties for us.

At the start of the second half our pack took over with some spectacular driving and mauling which often gained 40 or 50 yards and we were rewarded with Ward's fourth penalty and a try by Price. We stormed straight back onto the attack and had the temerity to take the lead with a drop goal from Ward. It hardly seemed possible after our hesitant play in the first half that, with ten minutes of the game left, we should be in the lead. We were within sight of a great victory – but it was not to be.

Some more wayward kicking when we needed to keep an iron grip on proceedings allowed South Africa to hit back twice and win. Germishuys gobbled up a weak kick-ahead and after some spirited inter-passing with Pienaar, Van Heerden and Louw, he scored himself. Botha converted to make it 22–19. Tony Ward squared the match with his fifth penalty to take his personal tally to 18 points – a record for a British Lion in a Test match. In injury time, we cracked again and Serfontein scored the winning try.

It is hard to argue with a try count of five to one against us, but our forwards were magnificent and did not deserve to lose. Had the kicking of the backs been better we would surely have won, but it would be grossly unfair to have blamed Tony Ward as he had only just arrived that week, was hopelessly short of match practice and did incredibly well to keep us in contention with his goal kicking. However, a defeat in injury time was scant reward for our superb forward display. It would not be an exaggeration to say that our forwards did enough to win the Test and the poor tactical kicking of the backs did enough to lose it. Already the alarm bells were clanging in my head, drawing depressing comparisons with the Lions in New Zealand in 1977.

The cloud created by the departure home of Mike Slemen had a silver lining because it gave us an opportunity to check on Andy Irvine's fitness and happily he was able to join the tour. With Andy the best attacking fullback in the UK, we now had the option to expand our game if we wished. If we decided to play ten-man percentage rugby, taking no chances, playing the game in our opponents' half and waiting for a handful of kicks at goal to come our way, we now had three exceptional place kickers in Irvine, Ward and Campbell.

We began our build-up to the second Test with a big win over South African Country Districts at Windhoek and then put 32 points on Transvaal. It was in that match we lost David Richards and, in the next game, on the Tuesday before the Test, we lost Terry Holmes in our hard-earned victory over Eastern Transvaal. Most of the credit for the fact that we only won 21–15 against far inferior opposition belongs to the referee Stoney Steenkamp. When the fickle finger of fate makes the award to the worst referee in the entire universe, then I firmly believe that J. J. A. Steenkamp should be right at the top of the list.

Nevertheless, we went into the second Test at Bloemfontein with nine wins in our first ten matches and the bonus of a running back division to support our rampant pack. With Slemen back home, Andy Irvine switching to fullback and Elgan Rees out of action for a month with damaged knee ligaments, we had to play Bruce Hay on the left wing. What he lacked in speed and elusiveness, he made up for with wholehearted defence. Only Colin Patterson and John Carleton remained from the backs who had played in the first Test and though the poor coach was virtually starting from scratch with a new back division, it looked a more positive selection on paper.

Once again, the Springboks were greatly indebted to the all-round talents of fullback Pienaar for inspiring them to take a 2-nil lead in the series. He had a major part to play in all four of their tries and scored the last one himself to cap a fine display. They opened the scoring after five minutes when Andy Irvine broke one of the cardinal rules of rugby – he failed to find touch from inside his own 22. Germishuys caught the ball, opened up and the sweeping movement ended with Louw scoring. Shortly afterwards we took the lead with a bulldozing try from John O'Driscoll, who ploughed through several would-be tacklers, and Gareth Davies converted. That lead was short lived. Stofberg took advantage of some poor covering and tackling by the Lions, and an amazing decision by the referee not to penalize Mordt, to score. Bruce Hay firmly tackled Ray Mordt and the referee, Francis Palmade, should have penalized him, but, to the surprise of everyone in the ground, he allowed Mordt to get back on his feet still clutching the ball and link with Morne du Plessis to put Stofberg over. This was the turning point of the second Test and the whole tour. Instead of the Lions being awarded a penalty and a chance to attack, South Africa were given 6 points when Botha landed the conversion. This was the only bad mistake Monsieur Palmade made in two Tests, but it could not have been more important. Botha also kicked two penalties before half time and Davies kicked one penalty for us, leaving South Africa 16–9 ahead at the interval.

At the start of the second half we narrowed the gap to 1 point with two penalties from Davies and Irvine and we could have taken the lead ten minutes from the end. Ollie Campbell came on to replace Gareth Davies and almost at once we were awarded a difficult penalty wide out from 40 yards. I probably should have given the kick to Irvine but, instead, I gave the ball to Campbell and he missed narrowly.

That miss left us still trailing and we began to throw the ball around and take chances in our desperation to win. The Springboks counterattacked to score two good tries. Pienaar made the first for Germishuys with a neat kick-ahead and he ran right through our entire side from near the halfway line to score the last himself. In injury time Ray Gravell scored an unconverted try for us, but it was too late. Again, like the first Test, it was a game we could have won, but we had a few vital moments of lost concentration in defence and failed to make the most of our chances in attack. As in New Zealand in 1977, our forwards were perhaps guilty of overdoing the rolling maul and the power driving in the set pieces; while we were so careful to produce only high-quality possession, we rarely actually produced quick ball which is what the backs really wanted.

No matter how we analysed the first and second Tests, it was our own fault that we lost both. We had our chances, but we kicked badly, failed to score when we should have, made a lot of careless errors which cost us points, and failed to force the Springboks into making the same sort of silly mistakes that we made. We probably should have had the confidence in those last ten minutes at Bloemfontein not to throw the ball about simply because we were trailing by 1 point. We should have continued to camp in their half and wait for a penalty or chink in the South African defensive wall to open up. We should have been more patient – our impetuosity cost us dear.

I was a bit worried after that match that I might have joined the walking, or rather limping, wounded because my right knee was twice its normal size. I had great difficulty in hobbling round, but a quick visit to Dr Noble, a specialist, cured the problem. He inserted a hypodermic needle into my knee joint and drained out a third of a pint of blood enabling me to play the following Saturday. He reckoned it would have taken three months to have drained away the excess fluid with physiotherapy.

We notched up two wins over the Junior Springboks and Northern Transvaal before we enjoyed a week's break in Durban. Paul Dodge had joined the party as a replacement for David Richards and he played well enough in both those provincial matches to win a place in the third Test. Paul is a strong defensive player, a good kicker and has a steadying, calming influence on those around him, which is exactly what we needed.

Some of the backs were demanding quicker ball from the set-piece play as well as from the loose, but Noel and I felt that the backs had lost their confidence and that it would be more beneficial to try to win the match almost exclusively through the forwards. With this in mind, we may have been wrong to drop John Carleton in favour of Clive Woodward because it meant Clive playing out of position on the wing. Clive, not used to the role of wing threequarter play, made one mistake which was to cost us the match.

Thanks to a try by Bruce Hay and two penalties from Ollie Campbell, we were leading 10–6 with ten minutes to go when Woodward chased across the pitch to tap a rolling ball into touch. It was a filthy day with heavy rain being driven across the ground by a howling gale and it must have been cold, lonely and depressing to be stuck out on the wing. Clive should have hacked the ball into kingdom come, but not only did he just side-foot it over the touch line and no more, he also then turned his back on proceedings and retreated. He should have stayed in the line-out until our players had arrived, but not being a regular wing he failed to do this. Germishuys grabbed the ball, took a quick throw to Stofberg, who gave it straight back to him, and Germishuys shot into the corner to score. In dreadful conditions, Botha converted to give South Africa victory by 12 points to 10.

That incident was one of the most frustrating I have ever encountered. I could see exactly what was going to happen 35 yards away as I pounded across the pitch. I knew what Germishuys was going to do but was absolutely powerless to stop him. For the third time in three Tests, it was our own fault that we lost. We narrowly failed to score three times when Andy Irvine dropped a scoring pass, when Colin Patterson took a wrong option near the line, and when Paul Dodge cut inside with a glaring overlap on the outside. To cap it all, we gave away that soft, silly try. In the three Tests the South Africans had made the most of their scoring opportunities – we had not. I now found myself in the unenviable position of trying to avoid becoming the first British Lions captain this century to lose every Test in South Africa.

Whenever I have been away on tour with England or playing away matches in Scotland, Ireland or France, I have always made a point of emphasizing to the boys at the team talk on the morning of the match and in the changing room just before kick-off that we wanted to be able to hold our heads high when we returned to Heathrow. Far too often we have walked through the terminal buildings with our heads down and our shoulders slumped. At our team meeting on the Monday after the Port Elizabeth Test I told the Lions that we could still salvage our honour and pride, and return at the end of our tour crippled by injuries with our heads held high if we won the final Test.

On the coach to that day's training session I addressed the entire party again and told them there was still a chance to finish with a flourish if we could beat the Barbarians in Durban – we did – if we beat Western Province in Cape Town – we did – Griqualand West in Kimberley – we did – and South Africa in the last match of the tour in Pretoria – we did. I stressed that in twenty years' time when people looked at the record books nobody would give a damn about all our injury problems; nobody would give a damn about the Springboks' winning try in the first Test coming in injury time; nobody would give a damn about Palmade's awful decision not to penalize Mordt in the second Test; and nobody would give a damn about Clive Woodward's one momentary lapse of concentration which gave the Springboks the third Test. There was absolutely no point in feeling sorry for ourselves or hard done by. We had given away three Tests and it was up to the whole squad to grit their teeth, buckle down to a fortnight's graft and win the last four matches. With renewed spirit and confidence we scored 85 points in the three provincial games left, including our highest total of the tour – 37 points against Western Province.

Of course, we could not possibly expect to achieve such a good run with our history and background without suffering another serious injury and Colin Patterson was the poor victim. He tore his knee ligaments very badly in the penultimate match, which ended his rugby career, and we had to send an SOS to bring Steve Smith out for the final Test to sit on the replacements' bench. He helped to lift our spirits with his inimitable brand of non-stop humour, and reconciled his 8000-mile round trip to Pretoria by saying that it was just what he wanted, the perfect place to spend a long weekend. He was also pleased because he claimed he would pass into history as a regular question in all sports quizzes – name the 1980 British Lions rugby player who never played for the British Lions.

The ground in Pretoria had happy memories for me as I had won there in 1979 with North West Counties and again with the Lions three weeks earlier when we had beaten Northern Transvaal. In the final team talk, great emphasis was placed on the need to steamroller the Springbok pack backwards all afternoon and, having sucked in their loose forwards after a series of aggressive drives, we would release our backs. After out-scrummaging them, driving them back at the line-out and keeping them on the defence with rolling mauls, we wanted to give our backs quick ball from the loose to let them run and show their skills. We wanted to go out with a bang and we succeeded.

Needless to say, we made it hard for ourselves because we should have sewn up the game by half time. We were well on top and camped deep in enemy territory but, uncharacteristically, Ollie Campbell missed several kicks at goal and after half an hour we were level at 3 all, Campbell and Botha each landing one penalty. We took the lead just before the interval when Clive Williams scored his only try of the tour after a rousing run by John O'Driscoll.

We had outplayed and outclassed the Springboks, but completely against the run of play they scored three times early in the second half. Willie du Plessis scored a try and Gysie Pienaar landed two mammoth penalties. We were trailing 13–7 and haunting memories of the first three Tests went flooding through my mind. But this time we increased the tempo, moved our game up a gear, tightened our defence and staged a final dramatic rally. Andy Irvine scored a try after good work by the forwards and then Ray Gravell, who had an outstanding match in the centre, sent John O'Driscoll charging over to score by the posts. Campbell converted and that was the final score – 17–13 to the Lions. Our pack had cleaned out the Springboks yet again, but we had lost the series 3–1. With a little bit of luck we might have won the series 3–1 or even 4–nil – but life is full of 'ifs' and 'maybes'.

In retrospect, I enjoyed the tour immensely. My only regret was the fact that we lost the series. I did my level best to help all thirty-eight players make the most of a golden opportunity and I think every one was glad and proud to be a member of the 1980 Lions. We had great fun on and off the field and for everyone it was the experience of a lifetime.

For me there was the added strain of being constantly chased by members of the media; I had to make myself available and take phone calls at any time. In a normal day I would take between ten and twenty phone calls from reporters all wanting different quotes and stories. To my surprise I began to enjoy these interviews and struck up a pleasant working relationship with the press. I was always honest and straightforward and we developed a mutual respect.

At training I always tried to lead by example. By giving my all twenty-four hours a day, I hoped to persuade others to follow suit. Obviously I was disappointed with the standard of our back play, but the lads played their hearts out and we were not beaten for want of trying.

During our free time there were many memorable expeditions to safari parks, to golf courses, down mines, up mountains in cable cars, and to various barbecues and parties. And the occasional private trip often proved the most rewarding of all. I remember going with John Robbie to a hospital for physically and mentally handicapped children in Cape Town and spending the most moving three or four hours there. The children were thrilled to see us and we spent a wonderful afternoon in their company. I talked for a long time to a nine-year-old girl who was born without any arms or legs. By incredible determination she had mastered five different languages and was fluent in them all. It was a truly uplifting experience and, in its own way, put our rugby problems in perspective.

On another occasion we went big-game hunting in Windhoek and I shot and killed a kudu. As it collapsed and died, I felt physically sick at what I had done. I know now that I could never again shoot at another animal as long as I live. It is these sort of experiences that help individuals to discover a little more about themselves and perhaps change their values.

I made lots of lasting friendships and got on particularly well with Ray Gravell. Ray was very excitable and just before the Orange Free State game he came over to me in the dressing room and promised that he would get his first bone-crunching tackle in early – even if it was late. These proved to be prophetic, if humorous, words. About ten seconds after his opposite number had passed the ball for the first time in the match, Ray knocked him into the middle of the following week. He was one of a host of great characters on the trip.

That list also includes Syd Miller and Noel Murphy. Syd was the original poacher turned game keeper and he did a superb job. He was a strong but fair man, who had the respect of everyone. Noel was every bit as commited as I was to making the tour a success and we shared those disappointments in the first three Tests together. We learned from our mistakes and he made a superhuman effort to coach us to victory in Pretoria. I was glad for Noel's sake that we delivered the goods in that final Test. It was the perfect end to a great tour and he celebrated, as a tee-totaller, with a few glasses of orange juice. Not that he was completely tee-total during the whole tour. One Sunday we were indulging ourselves in a drinking session and Noel was knocking back the orange juice as if there was no tomorrow. What he did not know was that Jeff Squire was doctoring each drink with an increasingly large measure of vodka. By the end Noel was plastered and legless. The next morning he couldn't understand why he had a blinding hangover and splitting headache. We could. Maurice Colclough, on the other hand, was not tee-total. Quite the reverse. My constant vigilance in supervising his drinking orgies led to his referring to me during the last six weeks of the tour as 'The Chief School Prefect', and he even went so far as to present me with a tee-shirt with this phrase printed on the front.

But every single individual played his part and I can honestly say it was the most enjoyable and happiest ten weeks of my life. We had our ups and downs, but we overcame all the problems to hit back and win the final Test. Every man jack of the 1980 Lions had every right to hold his head high when he walked through Heathrow at the end of our South African safari.

14

Captaincy

After England won the Grand Slam a lot of people came up to me and asked me what makes a successful captain. The answer is very easy – fifteen very good players. That, without any doubt, is the most important ingredient. The critics said that after three years in the job I personally had made great strides as a captain and that is how I was able to lead England to the Grand Slam. But, in fact, although I had improved a great deal in my tactical appreciation, the simple truth is that I was in charge of a much better team in 1980 than I was in 1978.

In many ways the easiest job I had as captain was to lead the British Lions because I was surrounded by most of the top thirty players in the British Isles and had nearly three months to work with them on tour. My trip was tragically much less straightforward than most Lions tours because of the absurd number of injuries we experienced and there were extra pressures involved in travelling abroad for three months on a major tour with all the eyes of the press following and reporting our every move.

Having said that, captaining the Lions is still a lot easier than captaining a club side. We had the distinct advantage of training every morning or afternoon with the full attendance of thirty players, less the walking wounded. Often the hardest task for a club captain is to maintain the enthusiasm of the players for ten months on the trot when, Cup matches apart, most games are fairly inconsequential affairs.

With the many diverse counter-attractions which society can put forward in the eighties, I'm afraid that slogging round a muddy pitch in bitter, cold, wet weather in the murky dark in mid-winter, when only a third of one's team mates have bothered to make the effort to turn up, is no longer absolutely irresistible, if, indeed, it ever was. The club captain has the unenviable job of trying to persuade and cajole an assortment of individuals from a sweeping cross-section of society that it is good for the soul to punish the body two evenings every week instead of taking life's soft and far more palatable options.

He himself must, of course, turn up for every training session; usually there is one committee meeting every week; bar duty and general administration on another evening; and he must be the last person to be carried out of the clubhouse every Saturday night. He has to organize the beer kitty, the monthly disco, the club tour, the annual dinner and a hundred and one other things. It is a thankless, selfless, demanding, but vitally important job. If he has any energy and breath left, he has to give a team talk on Saturday to a group of people, most of whom he has not seen since the previous Saturday.

It is a very time-consuming and very frustrating job to captain a club side but it can be both rewarding and satisfying. The challenge I would have enjoyed most if I had ever captained Fylde would have been to blend together a whole lot of individuals of varying levels of skill and widely diverse ambitions to play as a team. I would have enjoyed trying to sort out the problems of working out the various strengths and weaknesses of individuals to see how best we could mould a strong team.

Nevertheless, this sort of conflict was similar to the problem I faced when I took over the leadership of England in 1978. I was thrown in at the deep end because England was the first team I had captained since

I left school. To me, it was the greatest honour I could possibly imagine and I lost many hours' sleep worrying about whether I could do it justice. At the beginning of my ten years of office, and right through to the very end, I felt a special responsibility as captain. No matter how well I myself played in a match, if we lost that international I felt it reflected directly on me and I found defeat increasingly hard to live with. To play well for England was one thing, but to captain them to victory produced a magic all its own.

When England lost, I always took it terribly personally no matter how well or badly I had played myself, and I think my genuine feeling of total involvement spread through the team. I was best able to express myself and convey my feelings on the pitch or on the training field rather than in brilliant oratory. At training I always tried to set an example and if I was prepared to train to my absolute limit of physical endurance I felt it reasonable to expect everyone else at least to break sweat. If, perchance, the rest of the squad was prepared to burst through the pain barrier with me, then so much the better. All I ever tried to do as captain of England or of the Lions was to be a player's player. I trained and played for my team and I never asked any player to attempt anything that I was not prepared to do myself. I revelled in being in the thick of action throughout every match, at whatever level, and I hoped to inspire others to give 100 per cent too.

At England squad sessions I always felt it was important to be well organized and to plan in advance, and to this end I worked closely with the coach. There is nothing more soul destroying than to find coach and captain arguing during training about what to do or how to do it, or to find them at the start of a session asking the players if they have any ideas for training that night. Latterly, I would discuss training with Mike Davis or with Noel Murphy on the Lions tour at dinner the night before or at breakfast on the morning of the match and we would present a united front to the team with a detailed one-hour programme. Everyone knew what to expect and with everyone pulling in the same direction we got through a lot of work and developed our individual, unit and team skills.

It should be just the same at club level – there is nothing worse than hanging around half the night while everybody chips in a different idea about what it would be best to do at the next training session. With the coach, I always arranged a detailed programme which could last up to two hours, but we told the team what we were going to do and why, and we then had their support. At the same time I believe it is imperative for the captain to be one of the lads and in no way aloof from the team. The captain is no superior being in any shape or form and he should always muck in. The coach may or may not choose to distance himself a fraction from the team – but a good captain can never do that.

There are all sorts of arguments about what is the best position from which to captain a side. There is no conclusive answer, but I have found lock forward ideal. There is no better position from which to have a definitive view of the forward battle and to plan or change tactics accordingly. At every scrum I can feel exactly how the other fifteen forwards are faring and I know better than anyone what is happening in the line-out or in the loose. I can tell our halfbacks when to nurse our pack or when to stretch the opposition from side to side, and if I miss some of the finer points of the back play, I always have a pretty shrewd idea how the respective back divisions are playing by the direction I have to take to the breakdown after a set-piece. It is certainly easy to lead by example from lock and if I can lift the performance of our pack then I am making a big step in the right direction.

On the Lions tour with forwards from four different countries all thrown together for three months, it was pointless asking them to go out and have their heads kicked in or sacrifice everything to win the rucks and mauls if I was holding back to rush around in the open selling dummies. I had to be in the thick of the action, leading from the front and taking all the knocks that were going. I did this willingly and expected my men to do the same. The richest reward of all in South Africa was the fact that not a single player ever held back when the going got tough.

For England and for the Lions I tried to introduce a sense of realism into the team. I preached that there was no substitute for hard graft and the biggest problems arose when teams panicked. If our tactics were to play the match in the opposition half, which, at the highest level, they normally were, we had to work our way down there before throwing the ball about. It is very rare to run in tries from 90 yards at international level. The only reason teams try to run out of defence late in a game is because desperation teams panic when they are trailing. I tried to encourage teams to stick to sensible tactics and stay calm and relaxed even if we were losing and under intense pressure.

One of the problems I found at the highest level, though to an extent it applies at every level, was not cutting our suit according to our cloth. Ideally, the selectors should pick a side to do a particular job and the players should have the capacity to carry out that plan. I have already pointed out when that was not the case. When England decided to play a tight game which required a kicking fly half, the selectors picked a running fly half and we knew we were in trouble. To then insist on the poor fellow having to kick for eighty minutes – the thing he did worst of all – was suicidal in the extreme. I worked closely with Mike Davis and Noel Murphy to rationalize our approach. We examined the strengths and weaknesses of our side, analysed the strengths and weaknesses of our opponents and then decided how best we could win. It sounds blissfully simple, but I played in England sides in the mid seventies and for the 1977 Lions when this logical plan was certainly not pursued.

I was always prepared to listen to the views of the players on any controversial plan of action and would encourage the senior players, in particular, to air their ideas at team meetings. When I had heard enough different opinions, the coach and I would make the final decision and we had to be strong enough to get our views unanimously adopted. It is a bit like politics really – the Cabinet makes a decision and everyone has to support and propagate it whether he believes in it or not.

The captain's role off the field, of course, is to encourage harmony and build up team spirit and confidence, and the most important job is to make newcomers feel at ease. Quite often it takes a new player half a dozen matches before he feels he can play without overwhelming inhibitions; for my first two years in the team I expected to be dropped at any moment. I always made a special point of trying to help new players feel at home and looking after them as much as possible. If they were worried or nervous they were unlikely to produce their best form. Dave Rollitt's approach to me at my first trial, which I mention earlier – 'Who the hell are you?' – is not necessarily the best way to make a man feel relaxed, welcome, at ease and determined to follow Rollitt to hell and back.

I tried to arrange match tickets and tea tickets for new players so that their families were catered for and the players had nothing to worry about except the game itself. I would make a special point too of encouraging them during the game and congratulating them on every good piece of play I spotted early on to help them gain confidence. If a new centre put in a crunching tackle or a new fullback found a good touch, I would run past and say well done.

Too often young players are expected to prove themselves first before being fully accepted by the old campaigners. This is an old-fashioned, out-dated attitude that does a lot of harm because it inhibits the newcomers. There is a tendency for someone to be overcautious for the first few caps in the hope that if he does nothing wrong he will be retained in the team. This is a negative, but prevalent, attitude. I tried to encourage players to play their natural game on the positive basis that if they do something outstanding they will surely remain in the side.

I made a point of going round and checking on the general wellbeing of all the squad on the Thursday and Friday of England international weekends and would spend longer in the company of the new players to help them relax and feel an integral part of the team with a set job to perform. I would have an individual chat with all twenty-one members of the party at some stage before the kick-off.

It was important to spend most of that build-up period together to foster the spirit and morale. Apart from the training sessions, we would go en bloc to a film on the Thursday night or watch a video recording of a previous international match which featured the opponents we had to face that weekend. At the team meeting on Friday evening I left most of the talking to the coach. He would outline our tactical plan and with luck get us all thinking along the right lines for the Saturday afternoon. That was usually a short meeting and in 1980 we switched this from the Friday night to the Saturday morning. My feeling was that the team meeting got the adrenaline flowing and the blood pumping, but by the Saturday morning it had dissipated overnight. But a controlled four-hour build-up with Budge Rogers and Mike Davis beginning at eleven o'clock on the Saturday morning brought us nicely to fever pitch by three o'clock in the afternoon.

I preferred to save my own blood-and-thunder call-to-arms until shortly before the kick-off on the Saturday in the changing room. The ritual was much the same for every international match and similar even on the Lions tour. Players like the predictability of the routine and they fitted their own little quirks into the overall pattern. Since my retirement I have been unable to close my mind off from the Saturday morning scene during England's subsequent internationals. I can still picture

Steve Smith lying in bed in the untidiest room in the hotel watching 'Swap Shop' or 'Tiswas' and only getting up in the nick of time to attend the eleven o'clock meeting. At noon, Mike Slemen would flop into a hot bath to loosen off, and at the same time Phil Blakeway and Peter Wheeler would be out for a walk after a late breakfast discussing the match, this and that, nothing and everything. Usually about half the side would assemble in the room of Don Gatherer, our physio, to have a good rub down and to seek reassurance that this pull or that strain would stand up to eighty minutes of rugby. My second-row mucker, Maurice Colclough, would spend most of the morning on the phone clinching the odd £100,000 business deal in frantic cross-channel calls, and when he wasn't playing at being a tycoon he was playing at space invaders in the lobby of the hotel. Space invaders had a magnetic effect on several of the team with Maurice, Nick Jeavons, Nick Preston and Dusty Hare the most obsessive. As selling these machines was part of the Colclough business empire, he was a pretty red-hot player, but he faced some fierce competition from Nick Jeavons.

By the time 'Football Focus' came on television, most of the lads would be back in their rooms and many, like me, would be cleaning their boots so that at least we looked the part come the kick-off. The journey to the ground with a police escort took only a few minutes and on the way from the bus to the changing room Hilary would intercept me, wish me luck, tell me to play well and not get injured. Then we would pass through the changing room in a group on our way out to inspect the pitch. We would not actually bother to check that the posts and the white lines were there, but merely soak in the atmosphere and find out if the pitch was dry and which way the wind was blowing.

I always prefer to play into the wind in the first half and the huge majority of players in the England team and in the Lions teams shared that view. I found that the first twenty minutes of an international produced a lot of frenzied activity and a great deal of gamesmanship as individuals tested their opposite numbers, but there was very little fluent, controlled rugby. In the flurry and excitement of the opening exchanges, not a lot of constructive rugby took place and it was relatively easy to organize a solid defensive wall. Given the right attitude, it was not too difficult to contain a side if we were sufficiently well organized. That left us another twenty minutes to keep our line intact once the match had settled down, and then we had the final forty minutes to attack with the wind behind us once the overall pattern and style of the match had been established. It was also nice to know what target we were chasing at half time and then plan our tactics accordingly, although I was a simple enough soul to believe in the subtle strategy of belting the ball down wind and trying to camp in our opponents' 25 until the scoring opportunities came. This view would be considered heresy by most coaching manuals and by most coaches, but I certainly preferred to play into the wind and, despite what the selectors and press may like to think, most players supported me. If the wind changed round at half time, I would have been proved wrong, but I can't remember that ever happening to me.

The team photo was taken about twenty minutes before the kick-off and after that I asked everyone other than the fifteen players to leave the changing room as I took the warm-up and delivered my team talk at the same time. Psychologists in America claim that the fiercely emotional pep talk in the changing room has very little, if any, effect on an individual and merely goes in one ear and out the other, but I do not subscribe to that view. I found it an opportunity to work together as a team in the warm-up and cement a collective identity that would unite us on the pitch. I would go round every single player reminding him exactly what was at stake and what part I expected him to play in the match plan. Then we loosened off and warmed up together while I talked about the match and the honour we shared by wearing the white jersey of England. I would always point to the red rose and say how proud we should be that we have been chosen to represent our country. I would go over all the little things we had discussed during the previous forty-eight hours and we would finish off by gathering round in a big circle, holding each other tight while we did a couple of sprints linked together as a big happy family.

There are few greater pleasures in life, however transient, than leading a team out of the tunnel onto the pitch in an international. I miss this enormously now. I used to feel immensely proud as we stood in the middle of the pitch in a tight group for the National Anthem and the whole team would sing. Even now the hair stands up on the back of my neck and the butterflies flutter in my stomach as I stand at Twickenham whenever the National Anthem is being played. It reminds me of all the times I stood out there sharing a whole gamut of emotions with my men.

If things went well, I would encourage everyone to maintain and even increase his concentration and effort. If the game was going badly, I would try to be a calming influence and try to stop players from panicking. With the close relationship I tried to have with every player in the team, I knew who would respond to a bollocking and who needed to be reassured and encouraged when things were going wrong. I tried to look after them all and bring the best out of them. It was my job to drive the boys to the limit of their ability and to do it in the nicest possible way.

At half time I would change the tactics if necessary as I did in the final Test in South Africa with the Lions, or simply repeat our plan and ask for a renewed and redoubled effort from everyone. The hardest half-time chat, if I can dare use that phrase, was at Twickenham against Australia in 1981 when Miss Erika Roe made her sensational topless appearance. I was standing on the halfway line looking in one direction and the other fourteen guys were looking straight through me or over my shoulder. Great mates like Smithy and Wheeler were ignoring every word I was saying. Eventually I looked round to see what the distraction or counter-attraction was – or should I say were? I must admit it was a fantastic sight – I could hardly blame the guys for allowing their attention to wander. I quickly changed my tack. 'You see that half-naked lady prancing around on the goal line?' I had attracted the attention of my fourteen colleagues in a trice. 'Well,' I said, 'the only way you're going to get within striking range is by camping down there on the Australian line for the next forty minutes.' We proceeded to do just that and won the match.

After a game I would, without fail, go into the opposition changing room and talk about the match and make sure we parted on good terms for the reception and the dinner. On the way back to the hotel I would try to think of something witty to say in my speech that evening. I always found it easier to make a winning speech – a point I would impress on the team before the game. Captaining England and the Lions were both great thrills and there were great similarities between the two jobs.

I loved the responsibility and did my best, like an overprotective mother hen, to see that everyone was having a good time and, if not, to try to sort out the problems. In South Africa with the Lions I discouraged the formation of any cliques especially when several players from one country stuck together. I learned from the disasters of the Lions in New Zealand in 1977. I would go round the players' rooms to check on any complaints and arrange the rooming lists so that each person shared with someone new every three days when we changed hotels. I wanted the party to be integrated and friendly and I reckon we struck a very good balance in 1980.

I also believed I had a special responsibility as captain to set an example off the field; it would look very bad if I was found lying drunk in a gutter. I impressed on

England and on the Lions that we were ambassadors for our country and any misbehaviour of any description by one member would reflect on the whole party. I made it clear any offender would be directly answerable to me. I felt responsible for the actions of every player while we were abroad on tour and encouraged them to be polite, friendly and smartly dressed when we were invited to official functions or parties or club houses.

It was very time consuming and an enormous challenge, but it gave me great satisfaction and pleasure. Defeat felt twice as bad when I was captain, but victory felt twice as sweet.

15

Politics, Amateurism and Sponsorship

After I had been appointed captain of the 1980 British Lions for the controversial tour of South Africa, I expected to be inundated with letters and phone calls urging me not to go. In fact, I did not receive a single communication to that effect, but that did not stop certain sections of the media launching a campaign to have the tour called off.

My own position was made quite clear: I strongly opposed the policy of apartheid as practised in South Africa; just as I am strongly opposed to the persecution of dissidents in Russia; just as I am strongly opposed to the repressive political set-up in Argentina which denies human rights on a grand scale; just as I am strongly opposed to fascism and all other oppressive regimes which deny any semblance of justice and democracy.

But as long as Britain remains a democratic society, I would fight to my last breath to have the right to visit those countries if I so desired and to play against their sportsmen if I should choose to do so. To deny me that right is to deny democracy. The British government can, as Mrs Thatcher's government did, strongly advise our athletes not to go to Russia and our rugby players not to go to South Africa, but in the final analysis it must be left up to each and every individual to make his own decision. The Gleneagles Agreement, for what it is worth, explicitly urges Commonwealth governments to try to persuade sporting authorities and sportsmen not to have any links with South Africa. But that is as far as the Agreement goes. The respective governments have absolutely no powers of compulsion to stop such sporting links and that is exactly how it should be. They must try to dissuade, but in the end it is, quite rightly, up to the individual.

I saw and heard plenty in Argentina on my tour there with England in 1981 that alarmed me, but I would certainly be prepared to return there if I was invited by their rugby authorities. I would also be prepared to go to Moscow to play against the Russians and would be happy to play in Rumania. The whole ethos of selective morality is intolerable.

I deplore and condemn the whole notion of apartheid and everything it stands for in South Africa, but I still reserve the right to go there and play rugby if I so wish and, especially, as I honestly believe it does more good than harm. The Cape Coloureds, in particular, and most of the Blacks I talked to assured me that the policy of isolation was not the right one and they welcomed the Lions with open arms.

South Africa made giant strides in the seventies in a relatively short period. Already football, athletics and cricket have rapidly evolved into totally integrated multiracial sports. Rugby is gradually following suit and the pressures the Four Home Unions have exerted on the South African Board have helped to speed up the process. We demanded, and were given, several multi-racial fixtures which received vast media coverage throughout South Africa and these must have helped in their own way to break down the barriers and build more bridges for the future. Rugby has been going in the right direction in South Africa for the past ten years and it is my hope it will continue along the same path until rugby at all levels, including schools, is totally integrated.

Ten years ago no one would have believed a team of Whites, Blacks and Coloureds from South Africa would have played together against a British side. Although only on a limited scale, that has now happened and one can look forward with guarded optimism to more giant strides being made in the next ten years. I accept that there is still a long way to go, but it is my hope that once rugby at every level is completely multiracial in South Africa, the rest of society will soon follow this lead. Rugby players, as amateurs, playing for fun and enjoyment, should have the right to play against whomsoever they wish, wherever they wish. If rugby players have no influence or power to change a whole society, at least we have brought some pressure to bear on the organization of rugby in South Africa and it has made huge and dramatic advances as a consequence. A policy of isolation would have been less successful and that view is shared by Whites, Blacks and Cape Coloureds.

In 1980 the threat hanging over the heads of the British Lions was that we might jeopardize and ruin the Commonwealth Games in Brisbane in 1982 if we forged sporting links with South Africa. By going on the Lions tour we could deprive British athletes of the chance to participate in a great sporting occasion. But, of course, the corollary is also true. By cancelling our tour to South Africa and thus ensuring the Commonwealth Games were not disrupted, it would mean, indirectly, that the British athletes would, *de facto*, be responsible for depriving British rugby players of the chance to participate in an equally great sporting occasion.

The secretary of the South African Rugby Federation, Abie Williams, is a highly educated and enlightened man of his time. He is a Cape Coloured in charge of the administration of rugby for the Coloureds. He is a headmaster of a school in Cape Town, a friendly, intelligent, interesting man, whom I like and respect. He was adamant the Lions were right to tour and is keen to encourage further contact with top teams from the British Isles. He claimed it would have been a tragedy for South Africa if the Lions had not toured. He felt it was a huge step forward for the Lions to come up regularly against multiracial teams on that trip and it would do untold good for the sport and even society in South Africa.

We agreed that a large minority of South Africans are not helping the country march into the twentieth century by persisting in holding narrow-minded, out-dated views. Basically, the old, inveterate Afrikaner finds it impossible to change the ways of a lifetime and that is a great pity, but one day, sooner or later, he will see, or be forced to see, the light. Fortunately, the man at the helm, the guiding light of South African rugby, their president, Dr Danie Craven, is a man of rare insight and perception. He knows the progress which has undoubtedly been made in the past decade and is fully aware of the present limitations and the long road ahead. He is a gentleman and a scholar – South African rugby could not be in better hands.

The other thorny and pressing issues of the moment concern the rules on amateurism and the impact of sponsorship. The two are not totally unconnected.

I have always firmly believed that no one should ever receive any money for actually playing rugby. The game, in that sense, must remain strictly amateur. If players were ever to be paid for playing, it would ruin the game itself and the whole structure of rugby in Britain. I am confident I would have almost unanimous support for this view, but less confident of receiving universal backing for my other belief that once a player retires, he ought to be a free agent without losing his amateur status. Once he has played his last game I can see nothing wrong with him writing a book on his career or writing a coaching book and passing his experience on to youngsters.

To be branded a professional for announcing my intention to write this book only weeks after I had been regarded as a pillar of the Establishment seems quite ironic. The RFU know full well that I am exactly the same person I was before I wrote the book. My attitude to England and English rugby has not altered one iota and I am as intensely, passionately committed to

England as I ever was. I find it sad that I am now branded a professional for life and forbidden ever to coach or help in the administration of a club or county side – in short to put anything back into the game that has given me so much. Admittedly, only a tiny proportion of players would find it worth their while to write and publish a book, but these players comprise an imposing list at the moment and young people could learn a lot from the players who have recently been branded professionals – players such as Gareth Edwards, Phil Bennett, Ian McLauchlan, Fran Cotton and David Duckham. These players have all openly and honestly announced they have written a book for commercial gain and have been banned for life.

It is obviously a loss to the game that all the top players who have written books have subsequently been banned and I am sure that in the not too distant future this archaic law will be changed. I would like to see the International Board go further. Players once they have retired should be allowed to sell themselves in the commercial market. They should be allowed to advertise on television and in the Sunday colour supplements in the same way as other famous sporting personalities such as Henry Cooper and Kevin Keegan. Only a very small number of rugby players would receive commercial offers, but I feel that after their playing careers are over they all should be free agents, without putting in jeopardy their amateur status and their eligibility to coach.

I would argue fiercely that an individual should never be paid for playing, but I feel the RFU has often gone to extremes. It has often picked on petty items of expenditure during an international weekend and billed individuals for inconsequential items such as local phone calls. During my playing career I was well out of pocket by the end, but I would not have missed a single minute of it. However, a more rational attitude towards the financial burdens inflicted on top players would help. The daily allowance in Argentina in 1981 was laughably inadequate and just about covered the cost of one pint of beer. Players have often had to give up their jobs to represent their country on major tours and this whole area needs to be closely examined.

With the increase in the number of tours nowadays I find it quite understandable that some players are forced to make themselves unavailable. During the summer of 1982 nine of the top Australians were unable to tour New Zealand because of business commitments. There comes a time in almost all players' careers when they either have to stay at work to earn money or see their families suffer.

Sponsorship is the life blood of the game at the moment and as long as it is controlled I see nothing wrong with that. It is when it is not properly administered that the danger creeps in. Much has been written about players receiving money for wearing a certain make of boot or track suit. Figures of £4000 a year to a few important individuals have been freely bandied about in the last couple of years and for all I know they may be accurate. What I can say categorically is that I never made a single penny from any commercial concern for wearing its kit because I believe such a practice to be wrong for an amateur player. To accept money for advertising kit on the pitch is tantamount to being paid to play. However, there should be a firm dividing line between what a player can do while he is playing and what he should be allowed to do after he has retired.

The simplest way to end the rumours about underhand dealings between sports manufacturers and individual players is to have a similar arrangement to the one that has been used in New Zealand. The boot company should enter into a sponsorship agreement with the RFU, which would mean that for a certain sum of money paid by the firm to the RFU, all England teams would wear that company's boots in international matches. A considerable amount of money would then come into the game, and could be administered by the RFU for the good of rugby. The manufacturers would then have nothing to gain by approaching individuals and any temptation would be taken away from the players.

The main cause for concern at the moment is how to keep sponsorship discreet and acceptable. After I retired my farewell match at Fylde between two guest teams containing international players from all over Britain was sponsored by Diners Club. They paid all the travelling, hotel and administrative expenses, laid on stacks of food and drink, and contributed hugely to a wonderful day out. No players received any money, but they had a super weekend, and while there was no blatant, garish advertising, there were discreet reminders that the match had been supported by Diners Club. The organization had put up a marquee, invited selected guests to a banquet and to watch an entertaining game of rugby, and I was able to enjoy a memorable send-off thanks to its involvement.

I see no reason why club sides should not have all their home matches sponsored by different small businesses each week as Leicester, the most progressive club in England, does. The company sponsors the match, brings along its guests for lunch and tea, and hosts and guests watch the game, then mix with the players afterwards. It is an admirable arrangement and brings in welcome revenue for the club.

Now sponsorship money is being ploughed into the Five Nations Championship and, although each of the Home Unions is approaching this in a slightly different way, the end product will be much the same. Each Union will receive annually much more money than it has in the past. I should be delighted to see the bulk of this revenue devoted to promoting the game at grassroots level, but I should also like to see the players at the top looked after properly. No longer would it be acceptable to be told that we could not have a bottle of wine between four at dinner; no longer would it be necessary to stick tediously to *table d'hôte* menus; no longer would it be necessary to pay for our own laundry when away on a tour several thousand miles from

England; no longer would it be acceptable to be asked to find a pound for two or three local phone calls made from our hotel room; no longer would it be acceptable to be told that because we are bringing our wives to stay one night at our hotel we have to spend the entire weekend at a cheaper hotel. The incident to which I alluded in Chapter 10 is surely unnecessary nowadays. At international level players are largely responsible for bringing in gate receipts and sponsorship money of well in excess of a million pounds a year and I think they deserve the courtesy of receiving the best treatment. Sponsorship should help to ensure that state of affairs in the future without putting at risk the individuals' highly prized amateur status.

16

England's Wooden Spoon – 1983

The summer of 1982 was unusual in that, for the first time in a long time, I was not travelling abroad on a rugby tour. England went to America and Canada to prepare for the Five Nations' Championship and I went with Hilary to Ibiza to enjoy a holiday.

England stormed through North America, winning all eight matches comfortably, and the squad returned brim full of confidence for the new season. England and Scotland had warm-up games against Fiji, whilst Wales, showing far more imagination and foresight, had invited the New Zealand Maoris over for a six-match tour.

In the Cathay Pacific sevens tournament in Hong Kong the Fijians have been outstanding every year since this competition, far and away the best sevens tournament in the world, was inaugurated in 1976. They have regularly been finalists and have lost narrowly the last two years to the full Australian International seven in thrilling games. They are, indisputably, brilliant seven exponents who could match any country in the world, but sadly, they are not nearly so distinguished at the fifteen-a-side game and their tour in the autumn was a disastrous flop.

They lost every one of their ten matches because their forwards were simply not good enough to win enough possession to give their backs a decent chance. Although they are magnificent athletes and have the necessary physique, they are desperately lacking in forward technique and their burning desire to run with the ball was thwarted at top representative level by their inability to win sufficient possession either in the set-pieces or in the loose. They did, of course, provide plenty of flashes of their natural genius, grace, speed and remarkable handling ability, but they were unable to sustain these bursts of brilliance long enough to establish control in any match.

Understandably, the Scotland and England selectors purred with satisfaction after their respective victories over Fiji at Murrayfield and Twickenham in September and October, but such convincing wins against such moderate opposition only served to lull them into a fool's paradise.

Meanwhile, Wales experienced a thorough and searching test from the New Zealand Maoris and they emerged much better prepared for the Championship than either England or Scotland.

England had followed up their impressive wins over France and Wales at the end of the 1982 season with a string of facile and meaningless triumphs against Canada, America and Fiji. After annhiliating the junior side in the Trial at Twickenham in December England were installed as firm favourites to win the Championship and perhaps repeat the Grand Slam success of 1980. Two months later, their season in tatters without a single win in four internationals, the recriminations and investigations into the plight of English rugby began in earnest. The English representation in the British Lions party, announced in March, was lower than any of the other three countries, and all the confidence in the English camp, born of recent success, rapidly evaporated and completely disappeared.

The first cloud on the horizon appeared right at the start of the season when the selectors disregarded Mike Slemen. The best and most experienced left wing in English rugby was dropped after years of outstanding service without any opportunity to defend the left wing position he had filled with such distinction both for England and the Lions.

In one fell swoop, Budge Rogers and the rest of the selectors undermined the confidence of the national squad. If Slemen could be axed without even being offered a place in the Trial, then not one player could feel safe. It meant players immediately felt their own security of tenure was threatened, and with selectorial consistency ripped asunder, they once again had to play for themselves rather than for the team.

What compounded the felony, carried out, I'm sure, in all good faith by the selectors, was the glaring fact that there was no other left wing in England remotely as good as Slemen, even allowing for the fact that Slemen might not have been quite the player he was in 1980. To the astonishment of everyone, the selectors insisted on picking two players out of position to fill the huge void left by the omission of Slemen.

Tony Swift, who is an excellent right wing at Swansea, was selected on the left and, talented though Tony undoubtedly is, it was no real surprise that he looked uncomfortable playing out of position and failed to do himself justice. It was not his fault — the blame lay 100 per cent with the selectors.

After three undistinguished games, Swift was dropped and, showing staggering disregard for the blatantly obvious lessons they ought to have learned, the selectors chose David Trick for the final match of the season against Ireland. Trick, like Swift, has the potential to play international rugby on the right wing, but having confessed to a grand total of just one game on the left in his entire career he was in a hopeless position. It was a crazy decision by the selectors which was guaranteed to produce disastrous consequences, and that is exactly what happened. To pick players out of position might work occasionally at club level and, in my time, I dare say I could have survived the odd match at number eight for Fylde. However, the higher the standard the less probable it is that a player will perform well out of position. Any deficiencies are likely to surface at even county championship level and are certain to be cruelly exposed in international rugby. With Ollie Campbell in tactical control for Ireland, Trick was given a most difficult and unrewarding afternoon at Lansdowne Road, and his disillusionment spread right through the whole team.

The selectors, for whom I had such respect in 1980 because they displayed such commendable consistency when things were going so well, disappointed me in 1983 when everything started to go horribly wrong. They panicked, lost control and made a hash of selection which left their team totally bewildered and demoralized.

If left wing is perhaps not really the most important position on the rugby field, it could certainly be argued that either scrum half or fly-half is. Here again England dithered about in a most incompetent manner. Steve Smith was left bemused and confused by the Chairman of selectors Budge Rogers publicly criticizing him after the Welsh international. When all's said and done, he had just led England to their best result at Cardiff for twenty years even if he was guilty of the odd error of judgement, and the last thing the team needed was to have their captain pilloried by the selectors.

Ever since touring with Nigel Melville in Argentina in 1981, I have known that one day he would play for England and most deservedly so, but it is my firm conviction that England were quite wrong to drop Smith after Cardiff.

Considering, in retrospect, how well Wales did in the remainder of the season, England's performance can be seen in perspective. When Melville dropped out of the Scottish game through injury, the selectors found themselves in a most humiliating and embarrassing position because they had gone to the extreme lengths of choosing Nick Youngs as a replacement and not Smithy. The previous week, Budge Rogers told the press that if Nigel

Melville did not recover fitness in time, then Youngs would play.

Fortunately, common sense prevailed in the end and Smithy was duly recalled. However, such were the tactical restrictions placed on him by Budge Rogers against Scotland it is no surprise that he was not seen to the best advantage. For the second time in a fortnight he was dropped when the team to play Ireland was announced, but his fly-half partner, John Horton, surprisingly was retained despite an indifferent performance. Actually, when Cusworth was dropped for the Scottish match, it was crying out for the selectors to switch Huw Davies from centre to his rightful place at fly-half. Clive Woodward should then have been recalled to the centre to add some cutting edge to a somewhat blunt three-quarter line. There was certainly no evidence or logic to leave him out for that match and yet select him a fortnight later for Dublin.

Nevertheless, having eventually dropped Smith in favour of Youngs and recalled Woodward, it was surely quite bizarre not to recall Cusworth at fly-half instead of Horton. That would have given Youngs, at scrum half in his first international, his club fly-half with two more Leicester players in the centre and Dusty Hare at full back. It would have made a great deal of sense to choose all five Leicester backs and have a core around which to plan the game.

Dropping Smith meant a new captain had to be appointed for the last two matches. The obvious choice was Peter Wheeler, and I find it incomprehensible that he was overlooked. An outstanding captain of Leicester for many seasons and a great hooker for England and the British Lions, it was outrageous not to award him the highest honour in English rugby – an honour which he richly deserved. He, and he alone, just might have been able to organize and motivate England sufficiently to beat Scotland and Ireland, but, tragically, he was not given the opportunity.

John Scott was elected captain, and whilst I have

always thought that he had the right sort of ability, character and attitude to lead England one day, the middle of 1983 with the team in decline and on the slide was definitely not the time to promote him. Not for the first time in the last ten years we find English rugby at rock bottom securely anchored at the wrong end of the championship table.

Let me stress that having known, worked with and admired these selectors in the past, I know that every decision they made in 1983 would have genuinely been, in their view, in the best interests of England. They are a most energetic, enthusiastic 'gang of six' and I am sure, on reflection, they will willingly admit they made a mess of 1983.

In their defence, it should be pointed out that events conspired against them and presented them with a series of difficult and unforeseen problems. Phil Blakeway, the cornerstone of the pack at tight-head prop, suddenly announced his retirement early in the season to leave a gaping hole in the front row. At lock, Jim Sydall, who would have been an automatic choice all season, was sent off during a club match, and by the RFU's strict code of discipline, that meant he could not be considered for international rugby in 1983. If that was a severe blow, then the loss of Maurice Colclough with torn knee ligaments before half time in the opening international against France was utterly devastating. Instead of Colclough and Sydall throughout the campaign, England were left with Bainbridge and Boyle.

Having lost three of their anticipated first choice front five forwards, life was further complicated by the fact that John Scott, so often an inspiration at number eight, spent the year struggling desperately to find his best form. Of course, the selectors proceeded to exacerbate an already critical situation by lumping the extra burden and responsibility of captaincy on to Scotty. The last thing a great player who is out of form wants is to be saddled with the captaincy, especially when virtually the whole side expected, and wanted, Peter Wheeler to lead them. Not unexpectedly, being captain adversely affected Scotty in the last two games when he should have been free to concentrate on ensuring his own place in the Lions party, not trying to bring the best out of the other fourteen players in his team.

By the end of the season the players were bitterly disillusioned, and I have never know such a blatant rift between the players and the selectors. Tragically, Budge Rogers, the most well-meaning of men, had managed to alienate just about everyone, and there was precious little even a gifted and dedicated coach like Mike Davis could do. 1983 will go down in history as one of the worst years in English rugby. Mike Davis, a realist to the last, summed it up by saying England had performed their own impossible miracle – they had, in the space of a few months, turned wine into water.

Ireland, on the other hand, made the very best use of their resources, and showed enlightened loyalty to their team by picking the same fifteen players for all four internationals. Even after their defeat in Cardiff they sensibly kept faith with their team. The pack may have been showing signs of wear with virtually no one under the age of thirty, but technique, typically Irish fire and oodles of experience reaped rich rewards. With Ollie Campbell the tactical genius and gifted footballer at fly-half, they showed remarkable tenacity to beat Scotland and France narrowly, and their handsome win over England rightly earned them a share of the championship.

Scotland flattered to deceive and enjoyed their one moment of glory at Twickenham when they beat a thoroughly dispirited English side. The Scots were weak at lock, but an exceptionally good back row of Calder, Beattie and Leslie kept them in contention in every game. They lost three matches in close finishes by less than one score each which goes to emphasise the tight rope on which each international is precariously balanced and the narrow dividing line between success and failure.

Scotland were unlucky to be without Andy Irvine for the whole season after his ankle operation and also John Rutherford for the first three matches following his bad shoulder injury. With these two world-class players fully fit again the Scots can look forward to greater things in the future.

Wales can look back on 1983 with a great deal of satisfaction because, after beating the New Zealand Maoris in November, they only lost one match in the championship with a relatively untried and inexperienced side. In two key positions a couple of newcomers, Mark Wyatt at full back and Malcolm Dacey at fly-half improved with every game, and they repaid the patience and faith of the selectors with progressive performances of growing maturity.

Needless to say, Terry Holmes had another magnificent season and succeeded in spreading his considerable range of talents in a number of different directions. Not only did he nurse and guide his new fly-half through a torrid period of initiation when half of Wales were screaming for the recall of Gareth Davies, he found time to look after his pack by linking with them in a series of explosive bursts and by driving them forward with some brilliant line kicking. It is impossible to exaggerate the influence of this phenomenal player. Ackerman was their most direct and dangerous three-quarter in attack, and he was also their best and most positive defender, but the rest, at least, were all imbued with a certain ring of competence.

Up front, they introduced the most promising newcomer of the year in hooker Billy James, and Robert Norster quickly developed into the best lock in the championship. The loose forwards, after a hesitant start, looked an uncommonly useful combination by the end.

Eddie Butler turned out to be a good choice as captain and, largely by his inspiration and the efforts of the coaches, John Bevan and Terry Cobner, Wales came very close to finishing the season undefeated.

They fell at the last hurdle against France in Paris but

will be an even more formidable outfit next season. So, too, will France.

They appeared to be the best equipped all round side in Europe but staggered through the season with no recognized goal kickers and a moderate pair of half backs. Dospital, Dintrans and Paparemborde were the best front row in the championship, and Rives, Joinel and Rodriguez were, arguably, the best back row. But neither Berbizier nor Martinez at scrum half really capitalized on this solid and often sparkling platform, and much of the quality possession was squandered. Six of the French pack would have been automatic selections if they had been eligible for the British Lions, but none of the four half backs they tried would have been in the remotest danger of being chosen. Both Camberabero and Delage lacked the discipline, style and imagination needed at international level and, in consequence, a highly dangerous three-quarter line never really fulfilled its true potential.

At full back, Blanco confirmed all his abundant promise with a series of scintillating displays, and he was the most exciting runner in the five countries. With the likelihood that Galleon will return at scrum half in 1984, the French will have a dynamic back division if they can manage to unearth a decent fly-half from somewhere.

I would have relished my duties as a commentator with the BBC at the big internationals a lot more if England had had a better season. But I certainly don't begrudge France and Ireland their success. They deserved their share of the title. Wales did well to challenge so hard and finish just one point behind in third place, while Scotland were not to be denied their solitary major achievement in convincingly winning the Calcutta Cup. Equally convincingly and equally deservedly England won the Wooden Spoon. It would have been fitting at the end of a harrowing season for the players to have presented that Wooden Spoon to the selectors in recognition of their major contribution to their ultimate downfall.

17

Reflections

Whatever happened after the elation of the Grand Slam in 1980 was almost certain to be an anticlimax, and so it proved. My yearning ambition to win an international at Cardiff very nearly came to fruition, but Clive Woodward put his big toe a couple of inches off-side in injury time when we were clinging to a 19–18 lead and Steve Fenwick kicked the goal to give Wales a last-gasp victory in 1981.

We recovered from this defeat to beat Scotland and Ireland and we would have earned a share in the Championship if we had beaten France in the last match of the season. We might well have done just that but for an appalling decision by the Scottish referee Alan Hosie which wrongly gave the French 6 points. They won the match by 4 points to emulate our feat of the previous season by achieving the Grand Slam. Hosie must have known that he had made a real howler, but, unlike the incident at Stradey Park in 1980 during the Llanelli–New Zealand match when he ordered Graeme Higginson off the field for rough play and then was persuaded by players from both sides to allow Higginson to complete the game, on this occasion we raised no protest and he did not change his mind.

We had come perilously close to winning all four matches for the second year in succession and we set off in May on the most successful tour of Argentina ever by one of the four Home Unions. We became the first British country to win a series against Argentina and, considering we had lost Fran Cotton, Roger Uttley and Tony Neary from our pack and were missing a few experienced players who were unavailable, we did exceptionally well. We drew the first international and a week later decisively won the deciding Test to round off a pretty successful eighteen months for England.

I was only to be involved in two more internationals before my enforced retirement. In January 1982 we beat Australia at Twickenham and a fortnight later we drew with Scotland at Murrayfield to retain the Calcutta Cup for the sixth year in succession. This all goes to confirm that English rugby was in a much healthier state when I departed from the scene than it was when I arrived. In my first eight internationals I was only on the winning side once, but I was only on the losing side twice in my last twelve full internationals for England. Understandably, as I look back over my shoulder at the various highlights of my career, most of them, both on and off the field, took place in the last three seasons.

In February 1981, I was invited by Her Majesty the Queen to lunch at Buckingham Palace and this great honour reflected the success of the whole England side in 1980. The lunch was scheduled for the Thursday two days before the Scotland match. About a month beforehand I had had a telephone call from someone who claimed to be one of the Queen's private secretaries. He asked if I would like to have lunch with the Queen at Buckingham Palace; if I accepted, then he would send the invitation off in the post. I assumed it was one of the lads having a practical joke and I must confess I did not take him too seriously initially. After about half a dozen false starts in which I told him to stop messing about and be serious, I realized, to my embarrassment, that he really was phoning from the Palace. Naturally I said I would be thrilled to accept the invitation and it turned out to be a fabulous, unforgettable occasion.

One of the great moments in my life was climbing into a taxi at Hyde Park Corner and saying to the driver, 'Buckingham Palace.' We swept up to the Palace,

through the main gates and moments later there I was
– Bill Beaumont from Chorley – having lunch with the
Queen of England. I was immediately put at my ease
when the Queen began to talk about her visit to watch
the Welsh Centenary match when I had played for
England and Wales against Scotland and Ireland. She
remarked how much she had enjoyed the game, and
although I was absolutely petrified, a quivering bundle
of nerves, I managed to relax a little after that and really
enjoyed the next couple of hours.

There were a dozen guests there that afternoon and
I found myself chatting with Terry Duffy of the Engin-
eering Union, Sir Tasker Watkins, an eminent judge,
the Queen and Prince Philip. At one stage the subject
turned to the question of man management in industry.
At once the Queen brought me into the conversation by
saying that I must know something about that as captain
of the England rugby team. I was very impressed at the
way she was able to involve everyone in the discussions
and make each of us feel completely at ease.

At one point, Sir Tasker Watkins mentioned to me
that he was a keen rugby man and was president of
Glamorgan Wanderers. He wondered how Tony Simpson, a young flank forward who had played for his club,
was doing now he had joined Fylde. The next week at
training, I told Tony that Her Majesty Queen Elizabeth,
Prince Philip, Sir Tasker Watkins and I had been talking
about his rugby career over lunch at Buckingham Palace
and he nearly died laughing.

The meal was a veritable feast. The first course was
a superb seafood pancake with a rich cheese sauce on
top. As the butler stood there holding the enormous
silver salver in his spotless white gloves, I remember
having a terrible feeling I was going to make an awful
hash of serving myself. I decided to cut my losses and
rather than risk scooping up my pancake and cheese
sauce all at once with the heavy silver spoons, I scraped
all the cheese sauce off the pancake first so that I
wouldn't spill it or drip it all over my suit or over Dame

Josephine Barnes, a past president of the British Medical Association, who was seated beside me. It was an act of blatant cowardice, but in my anxious trembling state it probably prevented me from making a spectacle of myself.

When lunch was over, I hopped into another taxi and sped off to join the England team at our training session. The practice had already begun and I received a lot of good-hearted abuse for arriving late. The boys knew that I had been invited along to the Palace merely as their representative from our Grand Slam team.

If someone had told me ten years earlier that one day I would have lunch with the Queen in Buckingham Palace, I would have summoned the little black van to collect him and take him off for suitable treatment. If he had told me that within six months of that lunch I would also have attended a royal garden party at Buckingham Palace and have afternoon tea in the royal box at Wimbledon I would have had him instantly certified.

The Rugby Football Union always receive invitations to a garden party and that summer they passed a couple on to Hilary and myself. It was a very generous and much appreciated gesture. Strolling round the magnificent gardens and buildings at the Palace was a great once-in-a-lifetime experience.

A year later I again climbed into a taxi in central London and, for the third time in my life, I was able to ask the cabbie to take me to Buckingham Palace. I had been awarded an OBE and, along with Hilary and my parents, I was off to receive the award. I was thrilled to be given an OBE in the first place, but I could hardly believe my ears when the Queen said how nice it was to see me again as if I were quite a regular little visitor to the Palace. As she pinned the medal on me, she sympathized with my being forced to retire from the game and expressed the wish that this award might be some consolation. She chatted to me for quite a while and I was very touched that she was so interested in, and sympathetic towards, my retirement. It was a great moment for English rugby and I was intensely proud to receive the award on behalf of all the English players who had worked so hard to help us share the three most successful seasons England had enjoyed for twenty years.

As if the morning's ceremony was not enough excitement for one day, we sped to the House of Commons as guests for lunch of our two local MPs, Sir Walter Clegg of Fylde North and Edward Gardiner of Fylde South. We were joined there by the Minister for Sport, Mr Ian McFarlane, and I must say that although the MPs' canteen is not quite up to Buckingham Palace standards of *haute cuisine*, it was still very enjoyable.

In the summers of 1981 and 1982 I was invited along with Hilary to the royal box at Wimbledon to watch the tennis championships in style. They were two fantastic days out, not only watching the great players in action on the centre court but also meeting some outstanding personalities in the royal box. The Duke and Duchess of Kent have been marvellous hosts on each occasion and we have met Sir Douglas Bader, David Steel, the Liberal leader, Jackie Stewart and John Watson from the world of motor racing, and Fergus Slattery, Ireland's great rugby player.

None of the tennis players came up to the box while we were there, but Hilary, clutching her special royal box programme with the insignia on the front and sporting a smart ribbon, disappeared off to collect some autographs. She waited patiently outside the men's changing room and collected the signatures of Bjorn Borg, John McEnroe and Jimmy Connors. They all were happy to sign but on seeing the royal programme they kept glancing at Hilary, trying to work out which member of the royal family she was.

The other memory of our visit to Wimbledon was being asked by the waitress if we would like China, Indian or Russian tea. The tea was served in beautiful china and there was a superb selection of cakes and sandwiches. As we drove back to Chorley late that evening all the motorway service stations were closed except one and that was just a glorified transport café. We were desperate for a drink at the end of a long, hot, exhausting, but spectacular day. In we went, perhaps a shade overdressed for the occasion, and I ordered two cups of tea. Cups was not quite the appropriate word – two whopping great mugs were planted firmly on the counter before I had had a chance to consider whether to choose China, Indian or Russian tea. Our choice was a little more restricted than it had been during the afternoon! None the less, it still tasted pretty good and to have found this oasis in the desert proved the perfect end to a perfect day.

Since my retirement, I have been seconded by BBC Television to join their commentary team at the last two internationals of 1982. I thoroughly enjoyed working with Nigel Starmer-Smith in Paris for the England–France game and with Bill McLarren for the England–Wales match. I made a few clangers on the air, but I reckon it is much easier to play well in the commentary box than it is out on the pitch.

I was not too nervous about being wired up with a microphone because I have had a fair amount of experience doing 'Question of Sport' for the past two years with those great characters David Coleman and Willie Carson. I was furious to lose the deciding match to Willie in the play-off to find the winning team, but we had a tremendous lot of fun during the series and I'm looking forward to next year to gain my revenge. Although I enjoyed the quiz each evening, the great thing for me was meeting and chatting to so many top sporting personalities such as Ian Botham, Steve Davis and Kenny Dalglish.

Since I've retired I've managed to improve my water skiing and, coincidentally, my swimming, and for the first time in years the garden does not look completely neglected. I have learned to my disgust that railway weed really is a weed; this has come as a severe blow because I always thought it was a most attractive, pleasant little flower. The garden has certainly benefited from the amount of time I have on my hands now that I am no longer committed to training several nights a week and playing matches every Saturday and occasionally mid-week too.

Of course I miss rugby enormously. Nothing can adequately replace the thrill and excitement of the game at club, county and international level. Every match I watch I yearn to be out on the pitch playing and I find it tough to accept that I can never again play the game that has meant so much to me over the past twenty years. During all that time it has been much more than just a game, it has been an entire way of life. I have never given less than 100 per cent in training or in a match and I can honestly say that I have no regrets, although I would have liked two more seasons before being pensioned off. It has left a huge gap which will undoubtedly be very difficult, if not impossible, to fill. Hunting railway weed is all very well, but it does not offer quite such a stimulating challenge.

When I look back, I realize and appreciate how incredibly fortunate I have been throughout my career. I have been lucky enough to have had every conceivable break that was going. How many people win their first cap as a last-minute replacement when the first-choice player ricks his back bending down to pick up a piece of apple pie at lunch? I came to the England captaincy almost by chance and, blessed with the most gifted England side for many years, we won the Grand Slam two months before the British Lions tour to South Africa. With that shrewd bit of timing, I found myself thrust into the most highly prized job of all – captain of the Lions.

I have been lucky to have played with and against so many great players. I am intrigued by the number of people who ask me who were the best players I came across during my time in international rugby. I could spend another few chapters discussing the contrasting merits of dozens of outstanding players, but I think most people would really only be interested in my final selection. I have chosen what I consider to be the best fifteen players to have played for England during the period 1975–82, the best composite team from the 1977 and 1980 Lions tours, and the best World XV from all the people I came across between 1975 and the end of my career.

England XV

Dusty Hare
John Carleton
Paul Dodge
Clive Woodward
Mike Slemen
Alan Old
Steve Smith
Fran Cotton
Peter Wheeler
Phil Blakeway
Bill Beaumont
Maurice Colclough
Tony Neary
John Scott
Peter Dixon

British Lions XV

Andy Irvine (Scotland)
J. J. Williams (Wales)
Ian McGeechan (Scotland)
Mike Gibson (Ireland)
Mike Slemen (England)
Phil Bennett (Wales)
Terry Holmes (Wales)
Fran Cotton (England)
Peter Wheeler (England)
Graham Price (Wales)
Bill Beaumont (England)
Gordon Brown (Scotland)
Terry Cobner (Wales)
Derek Quinnell (Wales)
Tony Neary (England)

World XV

J. P. R. Williams (Wales)
Gerald Davies (Wales)
Bruce Robertson (New Zealand)
Roland Bertranne (France)
Brendan Moon (Australia)
Hugo Porta (Argentina)
Gareth Edwards (Wales)
Fran Cotton (England)
Peter Wheeler (England)
Graham Price (Wales)

Willie John McBride (Ireland)
Louis Moolman (South Africa)
Tony Neary (England)
Mervyn Davies (Wales)
Graham Mourie (New Zealand)

I daresay my teams will not be greeted with unanimous approval but it would be a sad world if we all had exactly the same views. These 35 players are the pick of the very best in my view – the *crème de la crème*. It was with rugby players at all levels that I shared some of the happiest moments of my life and I have had one hell of a time.

In looking at all the hundreds of pieces of memorabilia which I have neatly stored away in the inside pocket of my mind, half a dozen take pride of place. I shall particularly cherish playing my first game for Lancashire; the magnificent North of England victory over New Zealand at Otley; putting on the white jersey of England and running onto Landsdowne Road, Dublin, for my very first cap; my first win in an international and my first match for the Lions, as well as my first game as captain of England; leading England to the Grand Slam and captaining the Lions to victory in the fourth Test in South Africa; receiving the OBE at Buckingham Palace and having lunch with the Queen. I shall always remember with affection the fantastic tours I have had, the places I have visited all over the world – not just the major rugby countries like New Zealand, South Africa, Australia and Argentina, but also Japan, Fiji, Tonga and other exotic smaller places where the game of rugby flourishes.

Rugby, like life, is made up of good times and bad times and I shall also remember the bad times in the future. I won't forget losing seven of my first eight games for England, including the whitewash in 1976; losing the Test series in New Zealand and South Africa with the

Lions; losing to New Zealand at Twickenham in 1978 and 1979; being dropped by England after my first match and also having the captaincy taken away from me in 1978 for one match. I would not have missed any of these disappointments because they were all vital, integral parts of my career and helped to mould me into a better character and a more determined player. At various times of my career I scaled the heights and tasted the nectar of the gods; I have also plumbed the depths and felt utter despair. Success when it came would not have meant nearly so much without all the failures with which to compare it.

Win or lose, I have had some great times on and off the field and there is no other major sport, with the possible exception of cricket, which forges such long-lasting friendships amongst both team mates and opponents. At the end of the day my one abiding memory will be the unparalleled rapport between players the world over. It is a hard, physical game, but precious few players ever bear grudges and I hardly ever encountered personal animosity in a decade of senior rugby. Rough and tough the odd match may have been, but a few beers later we appreciated that we all had one thing in common – we were all rugby players and we loved the game.

Rugby has been very good to me and I have loved every minute of it – the ups and downs, the highs and lows, the triumphs and disasters. From humble beginnings on the playing fields at Cressbrook School, I have fulfilled my wildest dreams and greatest ambitions. I am eternally indebted to the greatest team sport of them all and I can think of no better way of concluding this chapter of my life than by saying thanks to rugby for ten unforgettable years because all the glitter, glamour and glory have only been possible thanks to rugby.

Career Record

Matches for England

Date	Opponents	Result	Venue
18.1.75	Ireland	Lost 12–9	Dublin
24.5.75	Australia	Lost 16–9	Sydney
31.5.75	Australia	Lost 30–21	Brisbane
3.1.76	Australia	Won 23–6	Twickenham
17.1.76	Wales	Lost 21–9	Twickenham
21.2.76	Scotland	Lost 22–12	Murrayfield
6.3.76	Ireland	Lost 13–12	Twickenham
20.3.76	France	Lost 30–9	Paris
8.1.77	Scotland	Won 26–6	Twickenham
5.2.77	Ireland	Won 4–0	Dublin
19.2.77	France	Lost 4–3	Twickenham
5.3.77	Wales	Lost 14–9	Cardiff
21.1.78	France*	Lost 15–6	Paris
4.2.78	Wales*	Lost 9–6	Twickenham
4.3.78	Scotland*	Won 15–0	Murrayfield
18.3.78	Ireland*	Won 15–9	Twickenham
25.11.78	New Zealand*	Lost 16–6	Twickenham
3.2.79	Scotland	Drawn 7–7	Twickenham
17.2.79	Ireland*	Lost 12–7	Dublin
3.3.79	France*	Won 7–6	Twickenham
17.3.79	Wales*	Lost 27–3	Cardiff
24.11.79	New Zealand*	Lost 10–9	Twickenham
19.1.80	Ireland*	Won 24–9	Twickenham
2.2.80	France*	Won 17–13	Paris
16.2.80	Wales*	Won 9–8	Twickenham

15.3.80	Scotland*	Won 30–18	Murrayfield
17.1.81	Wales*	Lost 21–19	Cardiff
21.2.81	Scotland*	Won 23–17	Twickenham
7.3.81	Ireland*	Won 10–6	Dublin
21.3.81	France*	Lost 16–12	Twickenham
30.5.81	Argentina*	Drawn 19–19	Buenos Aires
6.6.81	Argentina*	Won 12–6	Buenos Aires
2.1.82	Australia*	Won 15–11	Twickenham
16.1.82	Scotland*	Drawn 9–9	Murrayfield

*denotes captain

Test Matches for the British Lions

New Zealand

Date	Test	Result	Venue
9.7.77	Second	Won 13–9	Christchurch
30.7.77	Third	Lost 19–7	Dunedin
13.8.77	Fourth	Lost 10–9	Auckland

South Africa

Date	Test	Result	Venue
31.5.80	First	Lost 26–22	Cape Town
14.6.80	Second	Lost 26–19	Bloemfontein
28.6.80	Third	Lost 12–10	Port Elizabeth
12.7.80	Fourth	Won 17–13	Pretoria

In New Zealand I played nine matches for the Lions and scored one try.

In South Africa I played ten matches for the Lions – no points.

Other Arrow Books of interest:

THE ART OF COARSE RUGBY

Michael Green

Anything from 9 to 16 (never 15) physical wrecks dragging themselves out onto a freezing, misty pitch every Saturday afternoon to throw around a shapeless piece of leather. The object? To defeat a similarly-sized group of dead-beats with the least-possible expenditure of energy.

Here, in Michael Green's best-selling humorous classic, are all the fine points of the game of Coarse Rugby:

How best to take advantage of a blind, short-sighted or deaf referee.

How to sabotage your opponents' game through psychological warfare.

How to ensure that the visiting team lose their way before they get to your ground.

... And how to avoid paying for the beer afterwards.

£1.50

SPORTING FEVER

Michael Parkinson

Ever known a centre-half who could break coconuts with his head? Or a bowler that got bitten by his own false teeth?

Sporting fever runs in the blood. Michael Parkinson inherited the disease from a cricket-crazy grandfather who thought nothing of trudging thirty miles to see Yorkshire play, and it now looks as if his own children have fallen prey to it.

Bill Shankley, Gary Sobers and Muhammed Ali number among the sporting personalities Parkinson has watched, met or played against. But so do some other, less likely characters. . . .

'Parkinson is superb'   *Observer*

£1·25

THE PRIDE AND THE ANGUISH

Douglas Reeman

November 1941. Lieutenant Ralph Trewin, DSC, arrives at
Singapore as second-in-command of the shallow-draught
gunboat, HMS *Porcupine*. To Trewin, still shocked from
wounds received during the evacuation of Crete, the gunboat
and her five elderly consorts seem to symbolise the ignorance
and blind optimism he finds in Singapore. And the *Porcupine*'s
captain is as unwilling as the rest to take heed of Trewin's
alarm, for to him the gunboat represents his last chance.

The following month, the Japanese invade Malaya, and in
three months Singapore, the impregnable fortress, knows the
humiliation of surrender.

Through the misery and despair of this bloody campaign
Trewin and his captain are forced to draw on each other's
beliefs and weaknesses, and together they weld the little
gunboat into a symbol of bravery and pride.

£1.60

BESTSELLING NON-FICTION FROM ARROW

All these books are available from your bookshop or news-agent or you can order them direct. Just tick the titles you want and complete the form below.

☐	THE GREAT ESCAPE	Paul Brickhill	£1.60
☐	A RUMOR OF WAR	Philip Caputo	£1.95
☐	SS WEREWOLF	Charles Whiting	£1.50
☐	A LITTLE ZIT ON THE SIDE	Jasper Carrott	£1.25
☐	ART OF COARSE ACTING	Michael Green	£1.25
☐	UNLUCKIEST MAN IN THE WORLD	Mike Harding	£1.25
☐	DIARY OF A SOMEBODY	Christopher Matthew	£1.25
☐	TALES FROM A LONG ROOM	Peter Tinniswood	£1.50
☐	LOVE WITHOUT FEAR	Eustace Chesser	£1.50
☐	NO CHANGE	Wendy Cooper	£1.60
☐	MEN IN LOVE	Nancy Friday	£1.95

Postage —————

Total —————

ARROW BOOKS, BOOKSERVICE BY POST, PO BOX 29, DOUGLAS, ISLE OF MAN, BRITISH ISLES

Please enclose a cheque or postal order made out to Arrow Books Limited for the amount due including 10p per book for postage and packing for orders within the UK and 12p for overseas orders.

Please print clearly

NAME ....

ADDRESS ....

....

Whilst every effort is made to keep prices down and to keep popular books in print, Arrow Books cannot guarantee that prices will be the same as those advertised here or that the books will be available.